BENJAMIN FRANKLIN

Founder of the Library Company of Philadelphia. Copied from the original painting of J. S. Duplessis by Miss Anna Leslie.

BENJAMIN FRANKLIN'S LIBRARY

(Printed, 1936, as "The First American Library")

A short account of the
Library Company of Philadelphia

1731-1931

By AUSTIN K. GRAY
Librarian

With a Foreword by OWEN WISTER

THE MACMILLAN COMPANY
NEW YORK

IN MEMORIAM

———

JOHN CADWALADER

President of the Board of Directors

1932 - 1934

———

WILLIAM J. TAYLOR

President of the Board of Directors

1934 - 1935

iii

Preface

THIS book can only claim to lay out the materials for the history of one of the most interesting institutions in America. It was originally written in pamphlet form for the members of the Library Company. A real history of the Library would be a work of many hundred pages. It would in its way be an epitome of American letters from Colonial days through the Revolution and the Civil War to the present day. It would tell the story of books in America—their authors, their printers, their collectors, their readers—for a period of over two hundred years. And in the story many famous names occur—Franklin, Washington, Whitman, Poe from America, Talleyrand from France, Thackeray and Cobbett from England.

The materials for a history of the Library are scattered in many places and in many institutions other than the Library Company. They are also to be found tucked away in the memoirs and biographies of famous men and sometimes of men who were not famous. So far as record in the Library itself goes the chief authorities are the old *Minute Books*, the old stock catalogues, newspaper notices and a few odd letters. Less reliable have been found the innumerable histories and books about Philadelphia. There never was an institution that lent itself to legend so much as the Library Company and it has been difficult to sift legend from fact or to reconcile the contradictory statements of the annalists.

I wish to express my indebtedness to the short history of the Library Company written by my predecessor, Mr. George Maurice Abbot. Mr. Abbot was associated with the Library Company from 1863 to 1929. He was a treasury of legend, fact and tradition for its history. To Dr. Lawrence C. Wroth, of the John Carter Brown Library, to Mr. George Simpson Eddy, of New York, and to Mr. R. Dudley Edwards, of Rathgar, Dublin, I am grateful for elucidation and correction on some points in my first printing of this work. To Mr. David Knoblauch and Mr. John Govan of the Library staff I owe much information about books and people in the Library Company that can only come from long years of constant service on its behalf. To Professor Joseph E. Johnson, of Williams College, I owe thanks for much information about James Logan, the founder of the Loganian Library. Finally, I wish to thank the Grolier Club for allowing me to print the titles of the Americana procured from London in 1755, from the manuscript in Franklin's handwriting in their possession.

AUSTIN K. GRAY.

Table of Contents

Illustrations

Foreword

This account of what Benjamin Franklin called the mother of all such libraries in our country is written by its author with delicate and charming skill. From the days of Franklin's Junto when the idea of the library came to him, forty-five years before the Battle of Bunker Hill, through the winter when British soldiers availed themselves of the books, down to later times, the fortunes and vicissitudes of the ancient institution are set forth most engagingly. Because it was born in the Colonial days and because Philadelphia was the centre of national events from the Declaration of Independence to the administration of Adams, literary treasures and historic curiosities have fallen into the Library's venerable lap. To all Americans of intellectual and patriotic background this little book should prove a rare delight.

OWEN WISTER

I

THE JUNTO

A FREE press and a public library—those were two ideas that
William Penn brought with him when he came to American
shores to found his new commonwealth of Pennsylvania. They
were ideas that were common to most Quakers in England, but the
England of that time was not friendly to their growth. The press
came soon, for within five years of Penn's first arrival William
Bradford had set up shop and started printing calendars and works
of somewhat acrimonious religion. But not even in a New World were
the times ripe for full liberty of the press. Almost from the first
Bradford fell foul of authority. The Governor in Council denounced
him for printing the Charter of Pennsylvania; the Friends at Yearly
Meeting called in his almanacks for their "light, foolish and unsavoury
paragraphs." In the religious disputes that in those early days passed
for matters of statecraft, he sided with "the brats of Babylon" and
printed works propagating "Hatred and Heresie" and impugning the
Inner Light. For eight years he fought to print what he chose and
in the eighth year he was lodged in jail. Thereafter he forswore the
service of William Penn and departed in dudgeon to New York,
there to become, as he announced with an insolent flourish, "printer
to their Majesties King William and Queen Mary." And there, too,
he gave up printing works of religion and at last found peace.

The dream of a public library hung fire for many years. James
Logan, who came with Penn as his confidential agent and secretary
on his last visit to America in 1699, was a scholar and a lover of books.
Throughout the fifty years that he lived in Pennsylvania he imported
books for his own reading from England, France and Holland in many
languages. These books—over 2000 in number—he housed in a small
wooden building at the corner of Sixth and Walnut Streets, and members of the public, under proper guarantees, were allowed to consult
them and, in especial cases, to take them out. In his will Logan left
both building and books to the citizens of Philadelphia "in order
to prevail on them (as he phrased it), having such assistance, to ac-

1

quaint themselves with literature." This—the Loganian Library—
may perhaps be called the first attempt to create a public library in
America. But there was delay in putting Logan's wishes into effect,
and, in any case, a bright young man from New England had already
translated his ideas into practice by a different means.

Benjamin Franklin was a precocious boy of sixteen when he arrived
in Philadelphia, with a sharp tongue, an adventurous mind and, like
many a precocious boy before him, an ambition to set his views down
in print. He and his brother had been young intellectuals and radicals
in the last days of Mather theology in Boston. They had poked fun
at the elder bigwigs of their native city and then had fallen to blows,
in all senses of the word, with one another. Benjamin ran away from
home with vague ideas of becoming a literary character and writing
polite sarcasms about his fellow-men in the style of Addison's *Spectator*.
But in Philadelphia his ambitions underwent a change.

By comparison with Boston in the early twenties of the eighteenth
century Philadelphia was still a small and poor community. There
hangs in the Library a crude painting made by Peter Cooper of the
town as it was about 1720. It lay crouching beside the Delaware, a
conglomeration of red-brick houses with hardly a steeple or tower
above them to give the impression of a city. To landward it was still
cradled in woods and virgin forest that penetrated into the streets in
long avenues of trees. These streets were ill-kept and uneven of surface
and as they spread outwards into the country, most of them dwindled
into wagon-ruts and bridle-paths. Indians lurked in the woods and
on winter nights wolves howled under the windows of the houses on
the outskirts of the town. The centre of life and business lay along
the wharves and in the harbor where Cooper shows us innumerable
ships flying the Union Jack. But, small as the city was, there was a
freedom of mind in its air. It had left theological squabbles years
behind. Anglican and Quaker and Lutheran now dwelt side by side
in a spirit of more or less tolerant disapproval. The main preoccupa-
tion of most thinking members of the community was politics, prob-
lems of colonial administration and social economy, and under the
animating genius of Logan they had already turned their eyes in the
direction of natural science and philosophy. Franklin took his mental
color from his surroundings. His purely literary ambitions vanished
almost overnight and he slowly became the philosopher and statesman
that we know to-day.

At the instigation of the Governor, William Keith, he made his

A Short

DESCRIPTION

OF

Pennsilvania,

A Relation What things are known,
enjoyed, and like to be discovered in
in the said Province.

set as a Token of Good Will
of England.

By Richard Frame.

Printed and Sold by William Bradford *in*
Philadelphia, 1692.

RICHARD FRAME'S *A Short Description of Pennsilvania*
Pr. Philadelphia 1692. This volume, in the possession of the Library Company,
is the only existing copy of the first poem written and printed in Pennsylvania.

way to London and there, among other things, he learnt the principle
of the club. The intellectual life of England in those days—its politics,
its drama, its journals, its scientific societies—was fostered in coffee-
houses and nursed in tavern parlours and this secret Franklin brought
back with him to America. From that time onwards Philadelphia was
to be strewn with convivial clubs of his founding, which somewhat to
their surprise slowly matured into colleges, hospitals and philosophical
societies. In 1727 he established his first club in Philadelphia—the
Junto—sometimes called by the more genteel of its critics "the Leathern
Apron Club," because its members worked at their lowly jobs by day
clad in such vulgar and unmanly garb. It was a debating society—
part literary, part scientific. Every Friday evening its members met
in a tavern to discuss matters of morals, politics or natural philosophy.
As a body all the members had to promise to love mankind, respect
one another, believe in freedom of opinion and love truth for truth's
sake. As individuals each member had to contribute an essay once
every three months of a literary or scientific character. At first the
discussions were of an abstract nature (for example, what happened
to all the water that flowed into the Mediterranean Sea?) but in time
the Junto lifted up its voice in the political frays of the hour. Its
members favored the abolition of slavery and discussed the need for
a paper currency. In 1729 Franklin printed privately at his press
Ralph Sandiford's *Practice of the Times*, an abolitionist tract which
was handed out gratis on the streets of Philadelphia by its author.
Again in that same year, with characteristic caution, he issued from
his press anonymously his first work written in America—*A Modest
Enquiry into the Nature and Necessity of a Paper Currency*. The Governor of the State had favored the issue of paper-money some years
before; James Logan had opposed it, wherefore James Logan dubbed
the members of the Junto "the base and lying lackeys" of Sir William
Keith. Yet for all that he found "Ben" Franklin an "ingenious"
young man.

The members of the Junto were young and, with one exception,
poor. The exception to poverty was Robert Grace—"a young gentleman (Franklin tells us) of some fortune, generous, lively and witty;
a lover of punning and of his friends." The club desired more privacy
than a tavern could afford, so Grace kindly placed his house on Pewter
Platter Alley at its disposal. Franklin drew up the rules of discussion,
the most engaging of which was that, after a topic had been advanced
for consideration, there should be a pause "while one might fill and

drink a glass of wine." After Franklin and Grace the original members of the Junto were Joseph Breintnall, a poetical scrivener, Thomas Godfrey, a glazier with a genius for mathematics, Nicholas Scull, a surveyor, William Maugridge, a joiner, William Coleman, a merchant's clerk, William Parsons, a cobbler, and three of Franklin's friends of the printing-house, Hugh Meredith (his partner), George Webb and Stephen Potts. Later on other young men of modest calling and little wealth joined the club "for the sake of diversion, mutual aid and a rest from their wives."

The great lack of the Junto was books. Accordingly Franklin made a little proposition to the members assembled in "Pewter-Platter Hall." "Since our books were often referred to in our disquisitions on the queries", he writes in his *Autobiography*—"[I proposed that] it might be convenient to have them together where we met, that upon occasions they might be consulted; and by thus clubbing our books to a common library, we should while we liked it keep them together, have each of us the advantage of using the books of all the other members, which would be nearly as beneficial as if each owned the whole. It was liked and agreed to, and we filled one end of the room with such books as we could best spare. The number was not so great as we expected, and tho' they had been of great use, yet some inconvenience occurring for want of care of them, the collection, after about a year, was separated, and each took his books home again."

Franklin was not dismayed by first failure. It yielded, as usual with him, a new idea and it was the business of the world at large to match pennies with his ideas. "I now set on foot (he says) my first project of a public nature, that for a subscription library. I drew up proposals, got them put into form by our great scrivener, Brockden, and by the help of my friends of the Junto procured fifty subscribers of forty shillings each to begin with and ten shillings a year for fifty years, the term our company was to continue. We afterwards obtained a charter, the company being increased to one hundred; this was the mother of all North American subscription libraries, now so numerous."

His library, thus established, soon became a hobby with Franklin. While other young men gave their leisure to "taverns, games or frolicks," he set aside an hour or two every day to study "in Library," —to use his own phrase. There he read and made jottings from his reading on men, manners and himself. Some of these jottings are set down in his *Autobiography;* others, we may be sure, had ere that first seen the light of day in a *Poor Richard* almanack. He dreamed of founding yet another club—after the order of the monks of Thelema —to be called the "Free and Easy Club." His ambitions for his library soared and expanded. Other libraries would spring up, made in its image. Not only squires and merchants would learn to read with discrimination and so to think. Prentice-boys and farmers should become philosophers and seekers after knowledge by dint of reading books from subscription libraries and so, by sure degrees, judgment and independence of thought would penetrate into every corner of the state—into every corner of the whole wide continent.

II

BEGINNINGS OF THE LIBRARY COMPANY

THUS the Library Company of Philadelphia came into existence—
through the intellectual curiosity of a few young men, mainly
mechanics and clerks in stores, under the directing genius of Benjamin
Franklin, who was only twenty-five at the time of the Library's foundation. As the first of his projects of a public nature the Library
Company always held a high place in Franklin's affections, even after
colleges and hospitals and scientific societies had risen at the wave
of his wand; he served it faithfully and long in many capacities—as
Secretary, as Librarian, as agent in London, where all the toils of
diplomacy could not prevent him from hunting the bookshops in quest
of books to be sent home to the Library Company.

The first two things needful for this new venture were "the monies"
and the books. Franklin took the lead in procuring both. All the
original members of the Junto entered the Library Company with
the exception of Franklin's partner, Hugh Meredith, who had taken
to drink. The interest of the great James Logan was enlisted in the
cause and he, forgetting his former remarks on "lying lackeys,"
politely volunteered to give advice upon the choice of books. Lawyers
and doctors and professional men joined the fold—Dr. Thomas Cadwalader, author of a book on "the West India Dry-Gripes," Francis
Rawle, justice of the peace and writer on political economy, Thomas
Hopkinson, a young lawyer with scientific tastes but newly arrived
in Philadelphia from England. A Board of Directors was instituted,
consisting of Benjamin Franklin, Thomas Godfrey (inventor of the
Mariner's Quadrant), William Parsons, Robert Grace (all these of the
Junto), and Dr. Thomas Cadwalader, Thomas Hopkinson, Philip Syng,
Anthony Nicholas, John Jones and Isaac Penington. Joseph Breintnall (of the Junto) was appointed Secretary and William Coleman
(of the Junto) was made Treasurer. On November 8th, 1731, the
Directors met and Franklin urged that the "monies" of the first
twenty-five good men and true who had promised their support to
the Library, be promptly collected. It was arranged that three days

7

should be appointed for the collection of these "monies." Those who lived in town were to attend on the Treasurer at six o'clock in the evening on November 10th "at Nicholas Scull's." Those who lived out of town were to attend "at Owen Owen's" in the evening of November 22nd or 29th.

On November 10th ten gentlemen attended "at Nicholas Scull's" and paid over their "monies"—forty shillings for the price of a "share" in the Company and ten shillings for annual dues. An eleventh candidate for membership, Dr. Thomas Cadwalader, was "gone to sea", but had left his contribution with the Treasurer before sailing. The names are entered in the old Share-book in the order as follows—

1. *Robert Grace*	6. *Anthony Nicholas*
2. *Thomas Hopkinson*	7. *Thomas Godfrey*
3. *Benjamin Franklin*	8. *Joseph Stretch*
4. *John Jones*	9. *Philip Syng*
5. *Joseph Breintnall*	10. *John Sober*

11. *Thomas Cadwalader*

Two of the Directors, be it noted, had failed to pay—William Parsons and Isaac Penington. On November 22nd the following paid in their "monies" at Owen Owen's—

12. *Joseph Wharton*	18. *John Nichols*
13. *Nicholas Reddish*	19. *John Roberts*
14. *Richard Standley*	20. *Charles Read*
15. *Samuel Hale*	21. *Evan Morgan*
16. *David Bush*	22. *Thomas Edwards*
17. *Francis Richardson*	23. *Alexander Paxton*

On November 29th a solitary member—Rees Lloyd—appeared and paid up his monies to Benjamin Franklin, sitting at the Board table alone. On December 14th a straggler crept in under cover of night and paid—Benjamin Eastburn—and with him the first subscription list was closed. What reasons William Parsons among the Directors had for non-payment are not now known, but Isaac Penington sent word simply that he "lived in Bucks County" and left his excuse at that. Both gentlemen retrieved their good name upon a polite but peremptory mandate from Franklin. After New Year's Day, 1731–2, the doors were thrown open again and twenty-five more subscribers paid in their "monies." The Library Company thus started on its way with a capital of one hundred English pounds and an income from annual dues of twenty-five pounds a year.

The monies were now collected. The next step was the choice and purchase of books. At a meeting at Nicholas Scull's on March 29th,

JUNIPER-LOCUST STREET LIBRARY

Lea Hall, or Members' Room, built at the cost of Henry Charles Lea, the historian, 1888-9 (bust to right). The writing desk under the clock formerly belonged to William Penn.

1732, Thomas Godfrey announced that "Mr. Logan had let him know he would willingly give his Advice on the Choice of Books—he was desired to return the Thanks of the Committee (on books) to Mr. Logan for his generous Offer—and the Committee esteeming Mr. Logan to be a Gentleman of universal Learning, and the best Judge of Books in these Parts, ordered that Mr. Godfrey should wait on him and request him to favour them with a Catalogue of suitable Books." On March 31st, Robert Grace "to expedite the affair, offered to draw on his own Correspondent in London for such a Sum Sterling as would answer the Money in the Treasurer's Hands." Accordingly a Bill for Forty-five pounds (nearly half the Library's capital) on Peter Collinson, Mercer, in Gracious St., London, was sent to Thomas Hopkinson, together with a list of books ordered. The tendering of this bill was a solemn moment in the history of the Library Company. It was no light thing to order books from England in those days. Thoughtfully this Board of young men considered every possibility of disaster in their undertaking. Would Peter Collinson honor their draft? were there not storms at sea, shipwrecks and pirates? or maladies on shore? Suppose that Thomas Hopkinson were drowned? or died of a fever in far-off London? or that pirates carried the books captive to Algiers? Every danger was discussed and, where possible, every precaution taken against the hand of God, ere Hopkinson set sail.

Here is the list of the first books ordered, March 31st, 1732—

CATALOGUE OF BOOKS

Puffendorf's Introduc'n 8 vo.
Dr. Howell's History of ye World
  3 vols. Fo.
Rapin's History of England
  12 vols. 8 vo.
Salmon's Modern History
Vertot's Revolutions
Plutarch's Lives in small vol.
Stanley's Lives of ye Philosophers
Annals of Tacitus by Gordon
Collection of Voyages 6 vols.
Atlas Geogra. 5 vols. 4 to.
Gordon's Grammar
Brightland's English Grammar
Greenwood's " "
Johnson's History of Animals
Architect: by Andᵂ Palladio

Evelyn's Parallels of the ancient
  and modern Architecture
Bradley's Improvmt. of Husbandry
  and his other books of Gardening
Perkinson's Herball
Helvicius's Chronology
Wood's Institutes
Dechall's Euclid
L'Hospital's Conic Sections
Ozanam's Course of Mathem. 5 vols.
Hayes upon Fluxions
Keil's Astronomical Lectures
Drake's Anatomy
Sidney on Government
Cato's Letters
Sieur Du Port Royal moral essays
Crousay's Art of Thinking

CATALOGUE OF BOOKS—*Continued*

Spectator

Guardian

Tatler

Puffendorf's Laws of Nature etc.

Addison's Works in 12 mo.

Memorable Things of Socrates

Turkish Spy

Abridgmt. of Phil. Trans. 5 vols. 4 to.

Gravesend's Nat. Philos. 2 vols. 8 vo.

Boerhaave's Chemistry

The Compleat Tradesman

Bailey's Dictionary—the best

Homer's Iliad and Odyssey

Bayle's Critical Dictionary

Dryden's Virgil

Catalogues

This, to a modern mind, is a formidable list. Our forbears were in heavy earnest when they inaugurated the first public library in America. Dictionaries, grammars, history, books of facts and dates—that is what they crave. For the young and gay the only fare is the *Spectator*, the *Guardian* and the *Tatler*. Yet for the times it is a remarkable list. For note—there is not one work of theology in it. Any other city in America of that day—New York, Richmond or Boston, most of all—would have filled the list with heavy sermons and barren theomachies. For that absence we may in part thank the Quakers who gladly eschewed theology, and in part Ben Franklin, whose mind was eager for more curious studies. In place of theology we have Homer, Virgil and Plutarch and for that we may surely thank James Logan. In sober fact Logan's spirit of universal learning broods somewhat heavily over the whole catalogue—his interest in architecture, gardening, chemistry and, above all things, in mathematics and astronomy. Franklin for the nonce has withdrawn behind a greater luminary. We trace the *Spectator* to him, the *Memorable Things of Socrates*, the *Moral Essays* of Messieurs of Port Royal and Greenwood's *Grammar*, for he tells us in his *Autobiography* that these works greatly influenced him during his boyhood in Boston—particularly the *Memorable Things*, which taught him to confound his elders by means of the Socratic argument. And his practical Yankee taste peeps through for sure in the order for Daniel Defoe's *Compleat Tradesman*.

Thomas Hopkinson departed for England with the bill of exchange securely packed against his heart. From Dover on May 13th, 1732, he sent word to the Directors that his health—he thanked God!—was good. A week later he wrote from London notifying them that the bill of exchange had been honored by Peter Collinson. Towards the end of October Captain Cornock sailed into Philadelphia harbor bringing with him "the Library Trunk" full of books. They were

unpacked and placed on shelves in Pewter Platter Hall, which Robert
Grace had rented to the Company for a library building. Not all the
books ordered had Peter Collinson been able to procure, but by the
advice of Dr. Cadwalader and Thomas Hopkinson (both then in
London) he had made certain substitutions. He enclosed a gift of his
own—the first gift of books made to the Library—accompanied by
a very pleasing letter—

London, July 22nd, 1732

Gentlemen—I am a Stranger to most of you, but not to your
laudable Design to erect a public Library. I beg your Acceptance
of my Mite—Sr. Isaac Newton's Philosophy and Philip Miller's
Gardening Dictionary. It will be an instance of your Candour to
accept the Intention and good Will of the Giver, and not regard
the Meanness of the Gift. I wish you Success and am with much
Respect Yours—   Peter Collinson

Forthwith Benjamin Franklin dictated a letter of thanks to Peter
Collinson which Joseph Breintnall "copied fair" and despatched. Then
a Labelling Committee was appointed and Franklin undertook to
have a catalogue printed. The system of cataloguing and shelving hit
upon (for reasons unknown) was that employed in the Library of
Queens' College in Cambridge, England. This system holds good in
the Library Company to-day, though it has long since been abandoned in Queens' College. Its outstanding feature is that books are
catalogued under size first (folio, quarto, octavo) before such de-
tails as author and subject are considered. Some of his fellow-mem-
bers may have suspected that Franklin had reasons of his own for
wanting a catalogue printed, but they were agreeably disillusioned
when, being asked at the December meeting, 1732, what his charge
for printing the catalogues would be, he replied that "he designed
them for Presents (to each subscriber) and should make no Charge
for them."

The "monies" were collected, the books were on the shelves, the
catalogue was under way; now was the time to appoint a Librarian.
The choice fell upon a *protégé* of Franklin's—a young French refugee
recently arrived from Holland—Louis Timothée by name. Articles of
agreement were drawn up between Librarian and Directors. After
three months of probation Timothée was to receive a salary of "Three
Pounds lawful Money certain, and such a further Allowance as then
after . . . should be thought and concluded to be a reasonable Reward."

In return for his salary Timothée was "to give due Attendance in the Library on Wednesdays from Two to Three o'clock, and on Saturdays from the Hours of Ten till Four." He was to allow "any Civil Gentleman to peruse the Books of the Library in the Library Room, but shall not lend to, or suffer to be taken out of the Library by any Person who is not a Subscribing Member, any of the said Books, Mr. James Logan only excepted." As time went by new rules were added to the code. Slumber in the Library Room was considered a loud and offensive noise rather than a sign of decent repose, and the Librarian was instructed that "if any Person hath to be awakened Twice, he shall be requested to leave."

One last thing was necessary in order to inaugurate the Library as a self-respecting institution—the blessing of the sons of William Penn. On May 14th, 1733, the Directors met to consider the presentation of a humble address to the Honourable Thomas Penn, one of the Proprietaries of the Province, then recently arrived in Pennsylvania, with a view to obtaining his "Countenance and Protection in an affair so useful and well-intended as the Library." A Committee consisting of Franklin, Hopkinson, Coleman and Breintnall was appointed to draw up such an address and to present it for inspection by the other Directors the following evening. The address opened in fine style. "May it please your Honour—All the good people of Pennsylvania rejoice in your Arrival and Residence in this your Province, & will continue to rejoice in whatever promotes your Prosperity. Among the rest the Subscribers to the Library in Philadelphia beg leave to assure your Honour that in the same good Affections they are not behind the warmest of their Countrymen." From this noble prelude the document went on to say that Pennsylvania was happy in its climate, its constitution and its Proprietaries but less happy in the native genius of its people. To remedy that defect a "common Library" had been established, which surely deserved "the Countenance and Protection of a son of the great and good and ever memorable William Penn." Finally the address closed—"May your Philadelphia be the future Athens of America! May plenty of her Sons arise, qualified with Learning, Virtue and Politeness! . . . May every kind of human Felicity attend the Proprietary House, thro' all Ages to the latest Posterity!"

Joseph Breintnall notes in the *Minutes* that this address caused some shaking of the head among the Directors. Those that had "accustomed themselves to what is called the plain language" objected to

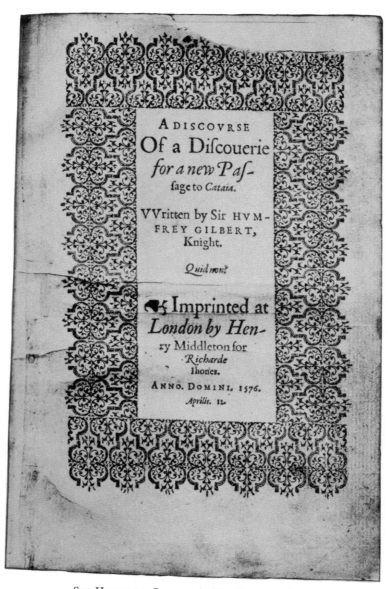

A DISCOVRSE
Of a Difcouerie
for a new Paf-
fage to *Cataia.*

VVritten by Sir HVM-
FREY GILBERT,
Knight.

Quid non?

Imprinted at
London by Hen-
ry Middleton for
Richarde
Ihones.
ANNO. DOMINI. 1576.
Aprilis. 12.

SIR HUMFREY GILBERT'S *New Passage to Cataia*
Pr. London 1576. A very rare item in *Americana*, purchased in London by
Benjamin Franklin for the Library Company.

the style as being too ornate, and moreover—was not Athens a heathen city? But "the Majority" (rendered vocal in Franklin, we suspect) pointed out that if the document were to be re-written in the language of the Friends, there would be delay and perhaps a complete alteration of the sentiments expressed. The address was accordingly presented without alteration to the Proprietary in person the next day by a deputation consisting of Franklin, William Rawle, Thomas Hopkinson and Dr. Cadwalader. The Proprietary received it "with great Civility and Kindness and was pleased to enquire some things concerning the Library." A few days later he sent for a list of its books and promised that in due course the Directors might expect a "Parcel" from his hands.

Thus launched upon its way the Library for the next few years proceeded upon a fairly uneventful voyage. The first catalogue was printed at Franklin's press in 1733. Louis Timothée (or Timothy, as he had now become) resigned as Librarian that same year and went to South Carolina to set up shop as a printer. To-day he is honorably remembered as the second printer of that State. Franklin succeeded him and held the office for three months and a day. To Franklin succeeded William Parsons, one of the Directors, who held office until 1746. In that year Robert Greenway was appointed Librarian. During his seventeen years' tenure of office the friendly relations between Directors and Librarian were disturbed. The Directors passed a by-law that the cost of all books lost from the Library should be stopped out of the Librarian's salary. Greenway protested vigorously; after all, he pointed out, it was the Shareholders and the Directors themselves who were most to blame for the loss of books by failure to return them. His protest was overruled and Greenway signified his displeasure by remaining away from the Directors' meetings. The Directors tried to enforce their by-law upon him whilst he still lived, out of his widow and estate after his death—with no success. This by-law, in deference to the Library Company's rooted aversion to change, still stands, but no attempt has been made to enforce it since Greenway's death.

The austerity of the first book-list was softened in later orders. Dictionaries, grammars and history continued to be the staple fare, but in the second list sent to Collinson (June 1st, 1733) the door was opened a crack to works of imagination; the poems of Dryden, Pope and that forgotten child of the Muses, the Rev. John Pomfret, were ordered. Later fiction reared its horrid head with *Robinson Crusoe* and *Gulliver's Travels*—this last, we suspect, by the advice of James Logan, who after long years of residence in Pennsylvania had learnt to admire the misanthropy of Swift. Individuals made presents of books. On March 3rd, 1733, an anonymous friend, dubbed in the *Minutes* "a transient Person," offered a book for sale to the Directors. A Committee sat upon the volume and reported—"'tis a Voyage to the South Sea and along the Coasts of Chili and Peru." It was bought for fifteen shillings. A few days later William Rawle presented "six vols. or Books of the Works of Mr. Edmund Spenser . . . the famous old English Poem called Spenser's Fairy Queen is included in these Works"—a gift which, after careful scrutiny for moral offence, was "kindly received." Louis Timothy presented "two old Manuscripts" in the Russian tongue, and Franklin gave Montaigne's *Essays* and a black-letter reprint of the Magna Charta (Lon. 1556).

The Directors met once a month at night to check the Librarian's accounts, to order new books, label old ones and pass upon applications for membership. Before many months were out that familiar problem of all libraries engaged their attention—the late return of books. Patiently and at length, in Committee and as a Board, did they discuss the case of Mr. Rees Lloyd, who had returned the *Travels of Cyrus* some days late—should he forfeit his note of hand for thirty-two shillings? There were tender souls who pleaded extenuating circumstances, but in the end the vote went for the rigor of the law. As a rule the Directors were firm about forfeiting notes of hand. Yet in defence of Mr. Lloyd and many another Shareholder who lived some miles away from the city, it must be said that it argued no small resolution on their part to drive their wagons into town to fetch Cato's *Letters* from the Library and bring back Ozanam's *Mathematics* in five volumes. They might sometimes have been excused for being late, especially in winter-time when the roads had vanished under mud and snow.

The Directors themselves were not always as punctual in attendance to their duties as Franklin or the Librarian could have wished. Ever fruitful in devices Franklin prevailed on them to submit to a fine of one shilling for non-attendance. This device increased the revenues of the Library but did not improve the attendance of the Directors. Franklin then hit upon another device. Every Director who was unable to attend the monthly meeting was, he ordained, to send a proxy in the shape of "two bottles of good wine." For a time this plan worked admirably. The Directors attended in force with great regularity—not, we may be sure, from motives of parsimony or prejudice against the consumption of wine, but in the hope that the other Directors would be represented by their proxies. But even that device lost vigor with time and in some years—in the eighteenth century—the bottles far outnumbered the Directors in the regularity of their appearance at the Board table. These meetings were held in eating-houses in the city, presided over by ladies who, by courtesy or misfortune, ranked as widows. The first of these benefactresses of the Library Company was the Widow Roberts. In 1746 she yielded place to the Widow Breintnall, in 1749 came the Widow Pratt and in 1757 the Widow Biddle. On June 13th, 1763, the reign of the Widows closed. The Widow Biddle notified the Directors that she "declined keeping a public House any longer," and the meetings henceforth were held at the *Indian Queen*.

In those days of Scotch pennies and doubtful moidores it was not always easy for would-be members of the Library Company to raise forty shillings sound money in payment of a share. The Directors, therefore, had sometimes to consider the advisability of permitting payment to be made by service or other means. Charles Brockden, the scrivener who drew up all legal documents for the Company, was awarded a share of stock in payment of his services. Others paid in kind. One gentleman obtained his share by presenting some stuffed snakes to the Library; a second gave a dead pelican; a third a set of skins, made into robes for former Indian Chiefs, which were hung on the walls of the library; a fourth presented an old cross-hilted sword dug up on his farm—a gift which led to much speculation on former inhabitants of the province; some thought the sword was Indian, others Spanish and yet others Roman. This practice of payment in kind continued throughout the century. In 1761, for example, Mr. Matthew Clarkson offered a set of fossils, received by legacy from his father-in-law, in payment of a share. A Committee sat upon his legacy at some length and reported to the Board that their knowledge of fossils was not such as to warrant them assessing their value in terms of cash. But Mr. Clarkson had his way. He was enrolled as a Shareholder and lived to be a Director. These various payments in kind were displayed in the Library and were known officially as "the Curiosities". It was one of the Librarian's duties to show them to strangers on a jaunt in Philadelphia, and in due time Mr. Clarkson's fossils were canonised in an essay by Tom Paine.

Slowly the Library increased in fame. George Whitefield, when he visited Philadelphia in 1740, made acquaintance with its books and its Shareholders. One of the Shareholders—Mr. Robert Bolton, a retired dancing master with a wife living and a young family—was so moved by "the divine preacher's" eloquence that he contributed his two eldest daughters to the orphanage that Whitefield later founded in Georgia. In memory of this and other benefits received from the Company Whitefield on his return to England had books sent to the Library. A yet greater preacher, John Wesley, somehow came to make friends with the Library Company and over a long period of years sent it books of his own authorship across the seas. There is a touch of drama in the fact that the last books to arrive at the Library from English shores before the outbreak of the Revolutionary War were a gift from John Wesley, the man who, against his will, led a great spiritual exodus from the Church of England. Presents of another kind than books came. Mr. Grey, M.P. for Colchester in England, sent "a noble Present of antient Medals." On June 18th, 1738, the Directors were astonished and delighted to receive a letter from Antigua, opening thus—"Sirs, the noble Design and most commendable Emulation of the young Gentlemen of your Province in erecting a public Library for the Advancement of Learning, promises so much Good to Mankind that I cannot withhold from contributing my Mite." The "Mite" was a bill of exchange for sixty pounds, worth in those days $1000—the first monetary gift to the Library. The donor of the "Mite" was Dr. Walter Sydserfe, an aged physician then resident in Antigua, whose memory should remain forever green in the annals of the Library Company.

One of the best friends that the Library Company ever had was Peter Collinson of Gracious St., London. This delightful Quaker, ardent antiquary and yet more ardent gardener, at once choleric and friendly, served the Library free of cost as its agent in London for nearly thirty years. The *Minutes* are strewn with his breezy letters. He was for ever sending gifts of books, plants and mechanical instruments. He preached the doctrine of the Library Company in London and prevailed on his Quaker friends—John Fothergill and others—to send presents. He was one of those men who could live robustly in his letters and needed not the bodily presence of a man to make him a friend and to quarrel with him. His forty years' correspondence with John Bartram, the Quaker botanist of Kingsessing outside Philadelphia (whom he never saw) is a bright interlude in the records of botany. The two friends exchange notes about flowers and trees in their far-distant gardens, they discuss the mysteries of "the sensitive Tippitiwichet" and quarrel only half in earnest about the respective merits of the Sweet White Narcissus and the Double Sweet Daffodil. In the end Peter Collinson could hold out no longer. On February 24th, 1743, he wrote to the Directors insisting that they make his friend Bartram a member of the Library Company. The Directors gladly accorded Bartram the full privileges of the Library, free of cost, and made him their second honorary member. Bartram showed his gratitude at his death by leaving several of his books to the Library, including those that he had received from the great Dutch botanist, Gronovius.

But what of the Proprietaries in these early years? Thomas Penn had accepted a catalogue and promised a parcel of books but, so far as record goes, the parcel never came. But Franklin never lost hope. In 1738 an approach was made once more, this time to John Penn in London. On January 31st, 1739, John Penn replied. He congratulated the Directors on being "the first that encouraged Knowledge and Learning" in his province of Pennsylvania and sent them, as the *Minutes* put it, "a noble Present of a costly—Air Pump!" With the Air Pump came one Mr. Samuel Jenkins, "a Gentleman well acquainted with Natural Knowledge and the Mathematics," who would instruct the Directors in the use of the Pump "which (so said John Penn) will be both natural and pleasant." The Directors accepted the gift with thanks. A meeting with Mr. Samuel Jenkins was arranged at the house of Thomas Mullen for May 8th, 1739, where, after due instruction in the use of the Pump, "the Gentlemen enjoyed a facetious agreable Conversation." The remains of John Penn's Air Pump may still be seen at the Library, housed in the wooden case designed for it by Franklin. The case is a magnificent specimen of the hand-carving and woodwork of Philadelphia carpenters in the early eighteenth century.

There was one service yet for the Proprietaries to perform for the Library Company and at length they saw the light and followed it. They gave the Company a tract of land on which to erect a library building, and on March 24th, 1742, they granted it a Charter. The tract of land was rented and in later years became a source of trouble, as the tenants were often behindhand with their rent. But with its Charter the Library Company blossomed forth as a full-blown corporation.

III

FROM THE CHARTER TO THE STAMP ACT

For thirty years after it had obtained its Charter the history of the Library Company was uneventful. The old Directors died or resigned, giving place to new. Thomas Godfrey, the inventor of the Mariner's Quadrant, gave place to Charles Thomson, later to be Clerk of the Continental Congress. William Rawle, first writer on political economy in America, gave place to John Dickinson, author of the *Farmer's Letters*. Thomas Hopkinson, the discoverer of the lightning-rod, gave place to his son, Francis Hopkinson, the Signer of the Declaration of Independence. The Rev. Richard Peters, Rector of Christ Church, was succeeded by the Rev. Jacob Duché, who offered up the first prayer in the Continental Congress. But Benjamin Franklin went on forever. He, the prime mover in the founding of the Library, outlived all his co-founders, all his friends of the Junto and his youth.

Pewter Platter Hall was soon found too small to contain the books and their attendant "Curiosities" and on April 7th, 1740, the Library was transferred "to the upper room of the western-most office of the State House" (now Independence Hall). Here it remained for close upon thirty-four years, serving in a measure as the library of the Provincial Assembly and the Supreme Court of Judicature. Jacob Duché in his *Observations on a Variety of Subjects* (Phila. 1774)—a series of letters about Philadelphia ostensibly written by a "Gentleman of Foreign Extraction" to noble lords and ladies in England and elsewhere—gives us a brief glimpse of the Library Company and its members in the days of its sojourn in the State House. After a description of "the majestic *Delaware*, compared with which our *Isis* and *Cherwell*, though immortalised in Song, would appear but little babbling brooks," and the beauty of the New Jersey woods on the further shore, he launches into a description of the State House, which he dubs "a large, plain building." In one of the wings, he continues, "which join the main building by means of a brick arcade, is deposited a valuable collection of books, belonging to a number of citizens, who are incorporated by the name of the Library Company of Philadelphia. To

19

this library I have free access by favour of my friend the merchant, who is one of the company. You would be astonished, my Lord, at the general taste for books, which prevails among all orders and ranks of people in this city. The Librarian assured me, that for one person of distinction and fortune, there were twenty tradesmen that frequented this library." This diffusion of reading among all classes in the State of Pennsylvania was a matter for comment from more than one alien observer, English or French. Franklin was proud of the reputation of his State in this respect and was fain to admit that the reading proclivities of his fellow Pennsylvanians might be due to the establishment of the Library Company in their midst.

On June 24th, 1771, the Directors applied for permission to erect a building of their own on State House Square, but the Provincial Assembly denied their request. Accordingly in December, 1773, they rented two rooms "in a new Building called the Carpenters' Hall, in the centre of the Square where the Friends' School stands." One of these rooms was allocated to the books which were now placed behind wire lattices for their better preservation. This was the public room and here the main business of the Library was transacted. In the days of Continental Congress and Revolution which soon after followed, it was a scene of much debate and yet more scribbling and writing of pamphlets. Men as famous and diverse as Benjamin Franklin, John Dickinson, John Adams, Tom Paine and William Bradford were often to be seen there in earnest converse by the book-shelves. In the other room the "Philosophical Apparatus"—that is, John Penn's Air Pump—was kept. In due course two other "philosophical" instruments were added to the treasures—always like "the Air Pump" referred to reverentially in the *Minutes* as "The Telescope" and "The Microscope." Shareholders brought their children to the Librarian to scan the neighbouring chimney pots through "the Telescope" or inspect dead flies under "the Microscope." Under strict oath individual members were allowed to take out "the Telescope" or "the Microscope," like a book, for the pursuit of scientific investigations in their own homes. David Rittenhouse, the astronomer, was a great borrower of both instruments for months at a time—"for repairs," said he. He joined the Library Company on August 14th, 1776—six weeks after the Declaration of Independence had been signed. The Telescope and the Microscope may have been one attraction for him in the Library. But he was also an avid reader of novels. Unfortunately for his studies in this branch of learning the importation of novels from England and Ireland—the only source of supply then available—had ceased some two years before the Declaration of Independence was signed. Was it, we ask, David Rittenhouse who originated that dark saying that is sometimes heard to-day when the supply of fiction runs short—"They never have any books at the Library Company"?

The Chamber of the Apparatus, the Telescope and the Microscope was used for the Directors' meetings and for their monthly dinner of oysters and punch—a meal that was taken, standing and hat on head, round a large wooden tub. The more impressive of the "Curiosities" adorned the room—stuffed birds, dead snakes, tomahawks—and it was hung with the robes of Indian Sachems. These tapestries, however, were later removed to a small closet adjacent to the Librarian's office and no one knows what happened to them after that. The earlier gift of skins which had hung round the walls of the Library in the State House had vanished in 1760. The Librarian—in August of that year—had complained to the Directors that these skins "grew extreamly offensive and troublesome." The Directors gave the matter serious thought. These invidious tapestries were a gift, a payment in kind from one of the Shareholders, wherefore they must act with circumspection to all concerned. They accordingly instructed the Secretary to notify the Librarian that he might remove only "such skins which are become thus offensive and troublesome." No more was heard from the Librarian on the matter and the fate of these earlier skins also remains an unsolved mystery in the Library's annals.

After the death of Robert Greenway there was difficulty in finding a man to assume the somewhat onerous responsibilities that the Directors had laid on the Librarian. At length Thomas Hopkinson's son, Francis, who had been serving as Secretary, undertook the job. Francis Hopkinson was in his youth Philadelphia's white-headed boy. He had been Provost Smith's favorite pupil at the newly founded College of Pennsylvania; with his two companions, Benjamin West and Thomas Godfrey, he had wandered beside the Schuylkill discoursing upon the future of art and letters in the American Colonies. Thomas Godfrey, the son of the inventor and founding father of the Library Company, met his death young as a soldier on duty in the Carolinas, but before he died he had won his place with his *Court of Fancy* as the first genuine poet of America and with his *Prince of Parthia* as its undoubted first playwright. Benjamin West lived to become the favorite painter of King George III of England, and Francis Hopkinson, having made his name as a writer of light verse and "ingenious" prose, crowned the promise of his youth by signing the Declaration of Independence.

Young Hopkinson embarked upon his career as Librarian with ideas of change and reform. Hitherto both Shareholders and general public had been allowed to take what books they wanted from the shelves for themselves. This practice had undoubtedly led to loss and damage. Realising that a by-law made him financially responsible for the loss of books, Hopkinson instituted the charging-desk (1764), whereby all persons wanting books had to get them out through the Librarian. This regulation caused "heavy displeasure" among the Shareholders and a protest was sent to the Directors. Various devices were considered for obviating the need for a charging-desk— for instance, it was proposed that any member wishing the freedom of the shelves should tender a bond whereby he made himself responsible for his proportionable part of any loss that might occur in books at the end of the year. But this and other proposals found no favor in the eyes of the Shareholders. A Special Meeting—the first— was called on August 27th, 1764. Franklin took the chair, supported by Edward Shippen, Joseph Morris and Jacob Shoemaker from the Directors, with Francis Hopkinson attending as Librarian and heavy villain in the piece. Four Shareholders in all came to the meeting— it would be better to say, as the *Minute Book* records, that two Shareholders came and two others sent their off-spring as their proxies —Isaac Paschal, Joseph King, "the Son of Mr. Hugh Roberts and the Son of Mr. John Biddle." After due discussion a compromise was reached. The charging-desk was retained; the freedom of the shelves was also retained. Yet more, the Librarian's salary was increased and members volunteered to assist him in rotation on Saturdays in giving out books. Lastly it was proposed that the general public should be excluded from the Library—an ordinance which was either never put into effect or promptly rescinded upon representations from the general public. In spite of his unexpected increase in pay Francis Hopkinson resigned as Librarian on May 13th, 1765, and resumed duty as Secretary. Benjamin Franklin, we make no doubt, went home smiling from the meeting.

The Library Company had lost the services of Peter Collinson in London in 1759—unfortunately by a quarrel. Collinson was in the habit of packing many things into "the Library Trunk" besides books for the Library Company—boxes of seeds, dried daffodils, microscopes for James Logan, leathern breeches for John Bartram, articles of more intimate clothing for Billy Boy (Bartram's son) and books for other people. Yet more, he would write to his friends in Philadelphia and bid them go round to the Library and bring home the good things awaiting them there. The Directors after nearly thirty years of tolerance rebelled against this practice and notified Peter Collinson briefly to that effect. On August 13th, 1759, they received a letter from Collinson "heavily complaining" of his treatment and resigning from his office of agent in London. Efforts were made at reconciliation. A letter was written by Francis Hopkinson, explaining that the original communication about the misuse of the "Library Trunk" had been "wrote in a hurry"; Franklin (when in London) was asked to see Collinson and try to mollify him. But in vain; Collinson remained implacable. He wrote one or two friendly letters to Francis Hopkinson in memory of his friendship with his father, but buy another book for the Library Company he would not. Eventually Franklin found "an honest and diligent bookseller" to take his place.

From 1757 onwards the Library catalogues show that the reading of the Library Company was slowly turning from instruction to entertainment. Poetry was gradually making its way in. Pope's *Essay on Man*—in the first edition—had led the way. In 1770 Goldsmith published his *Deserted Village* in London and the Library Company promptly bought a copy. From the novels of Richardson, Fielding and Smollett Philadelphians still averted their eyes, but Dr. Johnson's *Rasselas* was accepted and Goldsmith's *Vicar of Wakefield* and Sterne's *Sentimental Journey* (but not for a while *Tristram Shandy*). But the English novelist upon whom Philadelphians doted most was Henry Mackenzie, author of *The Man of Feeling* and other novels as windy as they are lachrymose. Even plays were admitted, such as Goldsmith's *Good-Natured Man* and *She Stoops to Conquer*, but we must remember that, whatever they wrote, Dr. Goldsmith and Dr. Johnson were always considered solid and respectable authors on both sides of the Atlantic in those days. In the eighteenth century there were, as to-day, robust Johnsonians in Philadelphia. Their leader was Colonel James Abercrombie with whom Boswell corresponded, and when Boswell sent him the second edition of his *Life of Johnson*, Abercrombie kindly gave away the first to the Library Company. Johnson's Dictionary was bought at once—in the year of its publication, and its arrival in due state is noted in the *Minutes*—December 6th, 1755, "Robert Greenway received into the Library Johnson's Dicty. 2 vols. Folio."

Not only books to read were now desired. Etchings and engravings were also asked for. On the news of Hogarth's death the Directors passed a motion that "a compleat set" of his works be ordered for the Library (May 14th, 1764). Franklin in London made himself responsible for obtaining these engravings. Direct from Hogarth's widow he purchased over one hundred and twenty specimens of her husband's work, including all the famous single pictures, the various progresses of the Rake and Harlot and divers bookplates. Francis Hopkinson went over to London and on December 14th, 1767, he returned, bringing with him not only the Hogarth engravings, but all the written works of Hogarth, a *Ruins of Athens* and "a Woman's Hand taken from an Egyptian Mummy in good Preservation presented with his respectful Compl<u>ts</u> to the Company by Mr. Benjamin West, formerly of this City, but now of London Historical Painter." These engravings, after one of them had been discreetly modified in the interests of the young person, were loaned out like books to the Shareholders. After three years of adorning the walls of Shareholders' houses for two weeks at a time or being thumbed and fingered by their off-spring, they were eventually withdrawn from circulation in 1770 and a duplicate set was procured from London. This set, too, began to show signs of wear and tear and in 1791 Boydell's edition of Hogarth's engravings was ordered to take its place. But the two original duplicate sets still survive, bound in heavy linen scrap-books.

For the increasing liveliness of its book-fare the Library has Franklin in part to thank. Although he had procured an honest bookseller in London to take care of the Library Company's orders, when he was in that city himself he took most of the work upon his own shoulders. The Directors often asked him to spend any balance left upon books that he might think suitable for the Library Company. Franklin made full use of the privilege and ransacked the London bookshops for books after his own heart. Sometimes a book about electrical experiments would find its way into the Library Trunk and next it would be a book about tides and little fishes. But most of all his fancy ran riot on what to-day we call *Americana*.

Even when he was at home Franklin (often with the connivance of Peter Collinson) intruded an extra finger into the pie when it came to procuring books from London. Every now and then a consignment arrived at the Library, not direct from Collinson, but through the medium of Franklin or his wife. A list of titles in Franklin's hand-writing would come with the books and, as like as not, it would con-

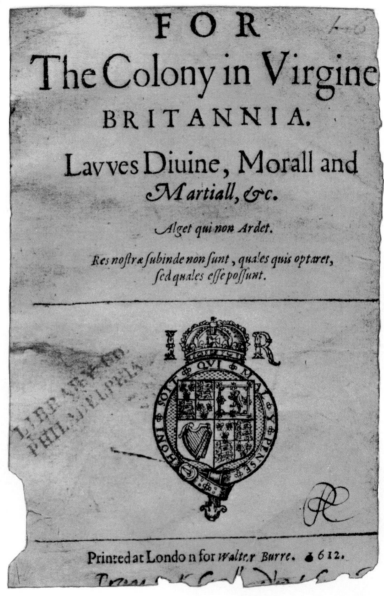

FOR
The Colony in Virgine
BRITANNIA.

Lavves Diuine, Morall and
Martiall, &c.

Alget qui non Ardet.

*Res nostræ subinde non sunt, quales quis optaret,
sed quales esse possunt.*

Printed at London for *Walter Burre.* 1612.

WILLIAM STRACHEY'S
For the Colony in Virginea Britannia

Pr. London, 1612. A rare item in *Americana*, procured for the Library Company by Benjamin Franklin from London, 1755. Peter Collinson, the Library's agent in London, has written his initials in the lower corner, right hand.

tain works not known to the Directors. On May 24th, 1755, for example, Franklin sent a trunk of nearly sixty books to the Library. The Directors had ordered a *Description of the North of Scotland* (2 vols.), a *New System of Agriculture*, some *Observations on Rocks and Stones near Bristol*, further *Observations on Bills of Mortality*, some *Letters concerning Taste*, some *Pleasures of the Imagination* and an *Enquiry into Homer*, and these worthy compilations had arrived in due form. But packed in among them were over twenty unwarranted half-bound books and unbound pamphlets, all concerned with the early history of the colonies—some of them with Peter Collinson's initials on the title-page. The catalogue of them in Franklin's handwriting is imperial in its sweep—from Acadia and Newfoundland in the north it travels over New England, Pennsylvania, New Jersey, Maryland, Virginia, North and South Carolina and Georgia to Guiana in the south. It is hard to estimate how much these works had cost Franklin (or rather the Library Company), but working on the law of averages for the price of other books, we might set the sum at £6 for the lot.

The secret of Collinson's initials on the title-pages is revealed in a letter that Franklin wrote on June 26th, 1755. The Library Company, he told his fellow-conspirator, had found these old accounts of the settlement of the colonies "very curious" and wished to return their hearty thanks to their good friend Collinson for his kindness in "sparing" them from his own stores. We cannot here give a full list of all the pamphlets that were thus smuggled into the Library. We will rest content with noting a few of the more outstanding titles—

Hakluyt.	*Virginia richly valued*	(Lon. 1609)
Johnson.	*New Life in Virginea*	(Lon. 1612)
Strachey.	*For the Colony in Virginea Lawes Divine and Morall*	(Lon. 1612)
Mourt.	*English Plantation at Plimoth in New England*	(Lon. 1622)
Capt. Smith.	*New Englands Trialls*	(Lon. 1622)
Morton.	*New Englands Canaan*	(Lon. 1637)
Plantagenet.	*Description of New Albion.*	(Lon. 1648)
Williams.	*Virginia the South Part richly and truly valued.*	(Lon. 1650)
Shrigley.	*True Relation of Virginia and Maryland*	(Lon. 1669)
Mather.	*History of the War with the Indians in New England.*	(Lon. 1676)

Hubbard.	*Narrative of the Troubles with the Indians in New England*	(Lon. 1676)
Anon.	*Declaration of the State of Virginia*	(Lon. 1610)
Anon.	*Declaration of the State in Virginia*	(Lon. 1620)
Anon.	*Virginia and Maryland*	(Lon. 1655)

Bibliophiles dream fondly of obtaining some of these books, but to obtain them all at one swoop for less than fifty dollars would rouse them from their slumbers with a glorious shout to the bleak realities of the book-collecting world. Not even the presence in the Library Trunk of Dr. Johnson's *Dictionary* in two volumes folio could abash Franklin. He it was, we may be sure, who arranged that that great work should be accompanied across the ocean by Hakluyt's *Voyages* (Lon. 1599–1600). Two years later he was back in London and Purchas' *His Pilgrimes* (Lon. 1625) followed Hakluyt, and then two books by that adventurous sailor, Capt. John Smith—*A Description of New England* (Lon. 1616) and his *True Travels and Adventures* (Lon. 1630). For some reason the Librarian hesitated to announce the arrival of these books to the Directors. When at last he broke the news he sought to mitigate the fact by announcing the arrival of Johnson's *Dictionary* a second time (1758)—as though those two portly volumes might serve as a chaperone for any vagabond pamphlets about the American plantations that had sneaked into the Library Trunk. The Directors instructed Mr. Peters to draw up a letter to be signed by all of them and sent to "Mr." Franklin. But protest availed not. Their colleague was incorrigible. He continued to pack the Library Trunk with trivial pamphlets about the settlement of America. And, as usual, he was right. These books, so little prized at the time, are now among the most valuable possessions of the Library Company.

IV

FROM THE STAMP ACT TO THE REPUBLIC

COMING events were casting their shadows before and the shadows fell across the quiet Library Room in Carpenters' Hall. The advent of the Stamp Act in 1765 awoke the English Colonies in America for the first time to a sense of national unity. There was a tempest of political pamphlets, some for, but most against, the government in England. Nowhere did the tempest rage more furiously than in Philadelphia. With the pamphlets went political cartoons and broadsides. Though the Stamp Act was killed the storm of pamphlets and broadsides once begun went on for over forty years—through the Continental Congress, the Declaration of Independence, the Revolutionary War and the presidencies of Washington, Adams and Jefferson. Over the Stamp Act the Whigs and Tories in England joined heartily in the battle on both sides and sent their pamphlets fluttering across the intervening seas. These authors, native and transatlantic, did not wish their works to be lost to posterity, so many of them presented their pamphlets to the Library Company. As a result the Library became in time a rich repository of all manner of publications dealing with the political life of the country from 1765 to 1800.

On August 31st, 1774, there comes a notable entry in the *Minutes* —"Upon Motion Ordered; that the Librarian (Francis Daymon) furnish the Gentlemen who are to meet in Congress in this City, with the use of such Books as they may have occasion for during their sitting, taking a Receipt for them. The Sect (William Attmore) is desired to deliver a Copy of this Minute to their Chairman." Soon after this meeting the delegates for the First Continental Congress arrived in the city by coach or wagon, by horse or carriage, from the four corners of the Colonies. On September 7th John Adams made the following note in his *Diary*—"At ten the delegates all met at the City Tavern, and walked to the Carpenters' Hall, where they took a view of the room, *and of the chamber where is an excellent library*; there is also a long entry where the gentlemen may walk, and a *convenient chamber opposite to the library*. The general cry was, that this was a good room, and the question was put, whether we were satisfied

27

with this room? and it passed in the affirmative." Mr. Peyton Randolph, Speaker of the Assembly of Virginia, was then voted into the chair as President of the Congress and word was sent to Mr. Charles Thomson, a member and one-time Director of the Library Company, to attend the meeting. Thomson was only three days married to a second wife and had come to town to pay his respects to his wife's aunt. "Just as I alighted in Chestnut Street (he says), the doorkeeper of Congress (then first met) accosted me with a message from them, requesting my presence. Surprised at this, and not able to divine why I was wanted, I however bade my servant put up the horse, and followed the messenger myself to the Carpenters' Hall and entered Congress. Here was indeed an august assembly! and deep thought and solemn anxiety were observable on their countenances! I walked up the aisle, and stopping opposite the President, I bowed, and told him I awaited his pleasure. He replied, Congress desire the favor of you, Sir, to take their minutes. I bowed in acquiescence and took my seat at the desk." Two days later another Director was called upon to play his part in the Continental Congress. The Rev. Jacob Duché opened the proceedings with a prayer which, Silas Deane wrote that night to his wife, "it was worth riding one hundred miles to hear. He read the Lessons of the day, which were accidentally extremely applicable, and then prayed without book about ten minutes so pertinently, and with such fervency, purity and sublimity of style and sentiment, and with such an apparent sensibility of the scenes and business before us, that even Quakers shed tears."

With the coming of the Continental Congress the Library Company took its place in the national life of the people of America. Peyton Randolph sent word to the Directors that the delegates would gladly use the Library's books and in the months to come they made full use of the privilege. The room where the Directors met was used as a Committee Room and the proceedings of Congress, in full session or in committee, were deposited in the Library. No less than eleven members of the Library Company served as delegates—Andrew Allen, John Dickinson, Benjamin Franklin, Thomas Mifflin, Robert Morris, John Morton, Samuel Rhoads, George Ross, James Wilson (Pennsylvania), Thomas McKean (Delaware) and Francis Hopkinson (New Jersey).

In the troubles of the years that followed, while the Old Country and the Young were inevitably drifting into war, the Library Company bore its share. The orders for books from London and Dublin

RIDGWAY BRANCH, INTERIOR

The Loganian Library is housed in the gallery. The bust of Minerva above the clock originally stood behind the Speaker's Chair in Congress. It was presented to the Library Company by Congress when it moved to Washington

came suddenly to an end and were not to be renewed for close upon nine years. As a consequence the Library had to fall back upon the products of the various home presses for intellectual sustenance and this sustenance for a long while was political in character. The meetings of the Directors were more and more sparsely attended. On July 9th, 1776, there comes an untidy scrawl in a new hand in the *Minute Book*—"Only two Directors present Viz!: Joseph Stansbury and Joseph Paschall no business was done." Even the most censorious critic cannot blame this poor attendance, for, five days before, the Declaration of Independence had been signed. With Benjamin Franklin leading, ten members of the Library Company were among the Signers— Robert Morris, Benjamin Rush, John Morton, George Clymer, James Smith, James Wilson, George Ross, Francis Hopkinson and Thomas McKean.

As the tide of battle rolled nearer Philadelphia the Librarian became anxious for the safe-keeping of the books. A Special Meeting of the Shareholders was called to consider the question of removing them to some safe place. Twice the meeting met, on May 31st and on June 6th, 1777, but owing to the general turmoil that filled the city, with enemy troops hovering on its outskirts, on neither occasion did the Shareholders attend in sufficient numbers to form a quorum. The books, therefore, stayed in Carpenters' Hall throughout the Revolutionary War.

Even before this alarm the Library had been called upon to play a strange part in the war. The city was full of sick and wounded soldiers and the two Library rooms were turned into an infirmary. In September, 1777, these soldiers had to be evacuated hastily from Carpenters' Hall and on the 26th of that month General Howe marched into Philadelphia at the head of the English troops. For the next nine months the city was under martial law—a gay martial law tempered by minuet and comedy—while Washington and his men froze all that long winter out at Valley Forge. The English officers made full use of the Library by taking out books on deposit. On the whole they conducted themselves discreetly and gave the Librarian little trouble. Though in these years of war several books were lost, stolen or damaged, little blame for that has been laid at their door. They returned books punctually and observed all the regulations about slumber and civility. Only one officer, a certain Major Trent—so far as record goes—failed to return a book when the English troops left Philadelphia in June, 1778. The book was Crantz's *History of Greenland* (Lon. 1767), two vols. Yet even that book was in the end returned to the Library—mysteriously from England in 1876—ninety-nine years after it had been taken out—surely the longest period for a book to stand as "overdue" on the records of any library and yet be returned.

Among the officers who frequented the Library were Sir John Wrottesley, Colonel O'Hara, Lord Cathcart and the romantic and ill-fated Major André. When General Howe resigned his command to Sir Henry Clinton, the famous ball and tournament known as the Meschianza were given in his honor. André was foremost among the designers of this gay medieval pageant and the books of the Library Company were ransacked for pictures and information about knights and chivalry, so that the rival ladies of the Burning Mountain and the Blended Rose might be entertained with old-world homage. Over a hundred years later (1889) many papers and relics of André were presented to the Library by the family of General John Meredith Read. They included the cotillion mirror used at the Meschianza Ball—a beautiful piece of woodwork—verses set to a German air by André, silhouettes and sketches made by him of his fellow officers and the Tory belles of Philadelphia—faded and pathetic memorials of a vanished epoch.

One man whom the British officers never met in the two library rooms in Carpenters' Hall was their compatriot Tom Paine, former stay-maker and exciseman. Paine had arrived in Philadelphia a few months after the meeting of the First Continental Congress. He found work with the newly-founded *Pennsylvania Magazine* and addressed himself heart and soul to preaching independence of the American Colonies from King George III. He was in and out of Carpenters' Hall, reading the Library's books and gathering material for his *Common Sense* and his many *Crises*, wherein he fought the battles of the Revolution with his pen. But when General Howe and the British troops marched into Philadelphia, he fled and took refuge with Washington at Valley Forge. There he still wrote pamphlets and exhorted "the summer soldiers and sunshine patriots" of Revolution to rally round Washington and oust the British troops from Philadelphia. He varied his pamphleteering activities by scouting along the lines of the enemy pickets and culling information from the occupied city. In due time the British troops marched out and the cause of American Independence triumphed. The years went by and Paine's talent for revolution found fresh scope in France. But Revolution under Washington and Franklin was a different thing from Revolution as fostered by men like Robespierre and Marat. Paine, who had defied King George in America, found himself pleading for the life of King Louis in France. His well-meaning philanthropy and his liberalism eventually earned him the enmity of the extremists. He was arrested, flung into prison in the Luxembourg Palace and marked by Robespierre for the guillotine.

In the meantime plump "Charlie" O'Hara, who had led the revelries at the Meschianza Ball, went on from promotion to promotion in the British Army. His military career was forever marked by respectable defeat and honorable captivity. He surrendered with Lord Cornwallis to Washington at Yorktown in 1781. Twelve years later he was, for his pains, a lieutenant-general in command of the British garrison at Toulon. There he was wounded and taken prisoner by the French troops under the command of a certain "little corporal" named Bonaparte. He was sent to Paris and lodged with Tom Paine in the Luxembourg. Paine fell sick of a brain-fever and the kindly Irishman nursed him through his illness. In the end Paine was saved from the guillotine by the downfall of Robespierre. On being set free from prison he procured the release of O'Hara in exchange for General Rochambeau. When the two men took farewell of one another O'Hara borrowed fifty pounds from his deliverer. Thus twenty years later Paine and O'Hara, who had fought one another unseen in America by pamphlet and medieval lance, met under the shadow of death in a jail in Paris and parted friends.

The British Occupation of Philadelphia and the Meschianza were a bright and unreal interlude in the history of the war and its brightest figure, André, later came by a sordid death. When Clinton and his troops marched out on June 18th, 1778, the city settled down once more to the humdrum and hardship of war. Even during the occupation the Library had managed to keep in touch with Congress and the struggle beyond the city borders. On July 8th, 1777, the few Directors left in town had met and renewed their offer of books to "the Gentlemen in Congress". One of the Shareholders, William Bradford, printed Washington's *Military Orders* and circulated them secretly through the city. Two of these fugitive broadsides yet survive in the Library, side by side with Sir William Howe's proclamations and the playbills of the "Military Thespians", who acted the comedies of Fletcher and Mrs. Centlivre at the old Southwark Theatre. But once the red coats and white perukes were gone, the Library's history was a dull tale. The cost of firewood was so high that the Library rooms were closed five days a week in the winter. In 1780 the Shareholders were ordered to pay their annual dues in bushels of wheat in place of the customary thirty shillings. A stray boat drifted into New York harbor, carrying books from London, and by the courtesy of Mr. James Rivington the Library Company was enabled to share in the loot. Otherwise no books came from London and few from elsewhere. One by one the Librarians drifted off to the war—there is a long procession of them all these years—Francis Daymon, Samuel Lobdill, John Todd, Bernard Fearis. In 1780 a permanent Librarian was found for a while in Joseph Fawcett, but he, too, suffered from suppressed military desires and grew careless of books. He lost them by the score and hundreds and those that escaped his talent for losing things lay, tattered, dogs-eared and unbound, about the Library room. One reason for this devastation may have been that Joseph Fawcett was absent for weeks at a time from his duties. In his absence the Library was administered by his assistant, one Isaac Brigs—"a lad of promising Genius," according to the *Minutes*, who had offered his services free in return for the privilege of reading the books. We should like to know more of this boy who held the Library together to the best of his ability during the Revolutionary War. Two years after the peace his superior, Fawcett, was discharged.

The signing of peace brought good times back to the Library. Almost at once the honest and diligent booksellers in London who had formerly had charge of the Company's orders, got in touch with the Directors and in the name of peace and good will solicited business after a long nine-years silence. The Directors looked up their last order for books on London and sent it with a bill of exchange for £200 from Robert Morris to Messrs. Woods and Dillwyn, of Billingsgate, London. With the order and the bill went a polite letter requesting those gentlemen to spend any balance that might be left over on modern publications that might, in their judgment, be useful for a public library. But, the letter concluded in warning, "tho we would wish to mix the *Utile* with the *Dulce*, we should not think it expedient to add to our present stock, anything in the *novel* way." A small trunk of books soon arrived from London—as fate would have it, in the good ship *Harmony*. It is interesting to note that among the first books to be ordered by the Library from London after the Revolutionary War was "Dr. Franklin's Works." In a later order of September, 1783, the Directors made up for lost time by ordering nearly

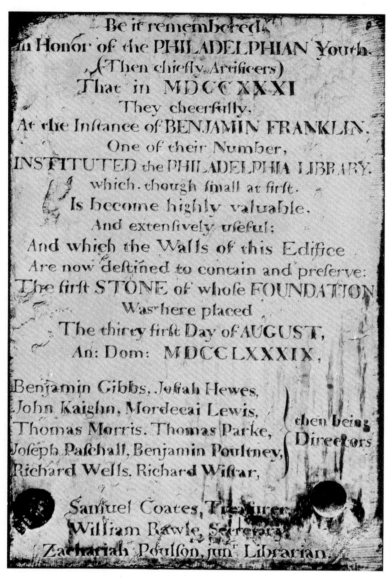

Be it remembered,
in Honor of the PHILADELPHIAN Youth,
(Then chiefly Artificers)
That in MDCCXXXI
They cheerfully,
At the Instance of BENJAMIN FRANKLIN,
One of their Number,
INSTITUTED the PHILADELPHIA LIBRARY,
which, though small at first,
Is become highly valuable,
And extensively useful:
And which the Walls of this Edifice
Are now destined to contain and preserve:
The first STONE of whose FOUNDATION
Was here placed
The thirty first Day of AUGUST,
An: Dom: MDCCLXXXIX,

Benjamin Gibbs, Josiah Hewes,
John Kaighn, Mordecai Lewis,
Thomas Morris, Thomas Parke,   then being
Joseph Paschall, Benjamin Poultney, Directors
Richard Wells, Richard Wistar,

Samuel Coates, Treasurer,
William Rawle, Secretary,
Zachariah Poulson, jun Librarian.

MEMORIAL STONE

to the original founders of the Library Company, set in the southwest corner of
the Old Fifth St. Library, August 31st, 1789. Franklin drew up the wording of the
inscription. He is not responsible for the two lines about himself. Those were added
by the Directors.

two hundred books from London—mainly biography, history, works about chemistry and electricity, and poetry—including under the last head Miss Seward's *Monody* for her dead lover, André.

Philadelphia had by now become the metropolis of the new republic. When Congress finally settled down to its meetings there the Library Company became the first Library of Congress. The Journals, Proceedings, Debates and other printed records of Congress were regularly deposited among its archives and have been so deposited ever since. The Library books were still available to "the Gentlemen of Congress," and the two first Presidents of the Republic—George Washington and John Adams—were elected honorary members of the Company with the privilege of using its books for life. Once more, in debate and committee while the Constitution was being framed, the Library Company played its part. On July 7th, 1787, the members of the Federal Convention returned thanks to the Directors for their "polite attention" in allowing them the use of the Library's books. And on Sept. 17th of that year six members of the Library Company subscribed their names to the second great State Paper of the American people —the Constitution of the United States. They were—Benjamin Franklin, Thomas Mifflin, Robert Morris, George Clymer, James Wilson and John Dickinson.

In 1783 the Directors had received somewhat curt notice from Carpenters' Hall that they must either pay double rent or quit the premises. The two rooms in Carpenters' Hall had long been inadequate for the growing needs of the Library. This notice, therefore, raised once more the question of erecting a permanent library building. In 1784 permission was asked from the Assembly a second time for a site on State House Square and was again refused. Overtures were made from the American Philosophical Society to join hands and besiege the Assembly for permission to erect two buildings, one for each society, facing one another on State House Square. But this move, too, led to nothing—indeed, in the end it seems to have produced some mysterious misunderstanding between the two societies upon the subject of windows and exposures—both sides, apparently, claimed the westering sun. Finally on June 1st, 1789, a meeting of the Shareholders was called under the chairmanship of Bishop White and a resolution was passed enabling the Directors to purchase a site and erect thereon a permanent building for the Library, so soon as one hundred new members had been added to the list. Eventually the Company purchased two adjacent lots, one from Mary Norris, the other from George Logan and Deborah, his wife, on Fifth St.

below Chestnut and thereon the first real home of the Library and its books was erected. No less a man than Thomas Jefferson submitted plans for the building, but in the end the architect chosen was William Thornton. He designed one of the most delightful buildings in old Philadelphia. It was square in shape with a Georgian classic front facing upon the street. Its walls were of familiar red brick with white window frames and white stone pilasters and pediment in front. A double flight of steps with an iron balustrade led up to the entrance door, and in a niche above the door stood a marble statue of Benjamin Franklin, presented to the Company by William Bingham, Esquire.

Franklin did not live to see the Library building completed. His affection for his first public project, the creation of his youth, never waned. For nearly sixty years he had in one way or another presided over its destinies, guiding it through its difficult beginnings and through times of stress and turmoil, with his incomparable spirit of good fellowship, his kindly bluntness of speech and a humorous wisdom in dealing with his fellow-men which at times amounted to a divine sense of fun. Before he died he had one more service that he wished to perform for the Library Company. He suggested that a stone should be laid at the southwest corner of the new building in memory of the young men (all of them, save him, long since dead) who had originally founded the Library Company. For this stone he designed the inscription as follows—

Be it remembered
In Honor of the PHILADELPHIAN Youth
(Then chiefly Artificers)
That in MDCCXXXI
They cheerfully
INSTITUTED the PHILADELPHIA LIBRARY
which tho' small at first,
Is become highly valuable
And extensively useful:
And which the Walls of this Edifice
Are now destined to contain and preserve;
The first STONE of whose FOUNDATION
Was here placed
The thirty first Day of AUGUST,
An: Dom: MDCCLXXXIX

That stone still stands. It is set in the wall of the present Library building, overlooking the small garden on Juniper St. Its inscription is Franklin's last message to the Library Company. In memory of his dead friends and of his own lost young manhood he wishes it two things for the long years to come—Cheerfulness and Youth.

V

THE FIRST FIFTY YEARS OF THE REPUBLIC

WHILE Congress met and Presidents lived there, Philadelphia ranked as the capital city of the infant Republic. For the first and last time in American history something in the nature of a court assembled round the First Executive—a select company of ladies and gentlemen who gracefully assumed responsibility for the destinies of a continent that lay sprawling in undiscovered forest and prairie at their back doors. Virginia squires and New England merchants rubbed shoulders on the streets. Envoys from foreign lands added a cosmopolitan note to the scene with their armorial coaches and old-fashioned wigs and brocade. Stately mansions, set in parks and formal gardens, rose along the hills above the Schuylkill—mansions built for elaborate entertainment, with pillared reception rooms and winding Piranesi staircases. The "beautiful Mrs. Bingham," who had known the great world of London in her youth, dispensed a sumptuous hospitality from her house on Chestnut St.—built in imitation of Montagu House in London, but, we are told, "twice as large." A lost fragrance from the desolate gardens of Versailles hovered in the air, brought over the ocean by refugees from the French Revolution. One of these exiles, the Duc de Liancourt, has recorded his impressions of Philadelphia at this time in its history; in elegance and luxury, he says, it recalled the capital cities and courts of Europe, only American women were, as a race, more beautiful than the great ladies of the old world. In these days of short-lived metropolitan splendor the Library Company stood proudly forth as the Library that served Congress—with Presidents and statesmen among its members. Its new home on Chestnut St. was only worthy of its new-born majesty. But when the capital moved to Washington, Philadelphia relapsed with a sigh into a long summer afternoon of quiet provincialism. And the Library Company relapsed with its parent city. Many names of men great in the records of Philadelphia as authors and scientists— Charles Brockden Brown, Caspar Wistar, Benjamin Smith Barton— figure among its members for the first fifty years of the nineteenth century, but of great names in the wider sweep of national life John

Marshall and Nicholas Biddle are, perhaps, the only ones. But during this period the Library grew rich in the benefactions of books.

Of outward history there is very little before the Civil War. On the evening of August 1st, 1793, the Directors met in the Fifth St. Library. The summer had started prematurely that year with flowers blossoming in the van of spring. All through May, June and July the weather had grown steadily more sultry and oppressive. This night of August was intolerably hot. The minutes of the meeting are transcribed by Benjamin Morgan with a tiresome fidelity to routine. The Directors were gathered in council to decide upon a date for a Special Meeting of the Shareholders. A crisis had arisen in the affairs of the Library Company. The Directors wished to abolish the vote by proxy at Annual Meetings. The Shareholders were prepared—by a lavish use of the proxy vote—to defend their privilege of voting *in absentia*. It seemed a well-nigh insoluble problem. The Board sat late, discussing ways and means. Finally the date was fixed for Aug. 30th at 6 p.m. But that meeting, so fraught with historic consequences, was never convened.

The next morning a stranger to the town, one Mr. Moore—his name, men said later, was the French for Death—returned to his lodging house on Water St., feeling faint and sick. He ascribed his illness to the stench of some rotting coffee that he had passed by on a wharf at the foot of Arch St. Within three days he was dead. A Mrs. Parkinson, lodging in the same house, died a day later of the same sickness. Then Mr. Denny, the owner of the house, died and his wife, and then two neighbours on Water St. Before the week was out the whole city lay paralysed in the grip of the Yellow Fever.

Scenes of horror and panic followed. The Hospital was crowded to overflowing with the sick, and the dead and dying lay in heaps in the yard outside. The church-bells tolled dismally all day and half the night long, until the Mayor gave out orders that they were to be silenced throughout the city. Bonfires were lighted in streets and open yards under the impression that somehow they appeased an angry God and might purify the fever-laden air. Over twenty thousand people fled from the city. From dawn to dusk there were long silent processions of refugees through the streets, escaping into the cleaner air of the country outside. Some went in carriages, some on horseback or in carts, others on foot, carrying all their worldly goods in linen bundles. Husbands left their dying wives, wives their dying husbands—even in the first days of honeymoon. Children were deserted

THE LOGANIAN LIBRARY

Old print, made from designs drawn up by James Logan, 1745.

on the streets and in empty houses. Thieves broke into abandoned dwellings and plundered and robbed, murdered the dying and fell dead in the streets with their plunder in their hands. As a last touch of horror a ship-load of French refugees, flying from revolution and massacre in San Domingo, arrived in the harbor. There were women and children on board; all were destitute and starving and many dying, yet, for fear that they should catch the sickness, the boat was marooned out mid-stream and only allowed to communicate with the city once or twice a week.

It is gratifying to record that a large number of Shareholders—with Matthew Carey, a Director, and Zachariah Poulson, the Librarian, at their head—distinguished themselves by their courage and industry in fighting the Yellow Fever. Many of them paid for their devotion with their lives. The Fifth St. Library was closed. Shareholders were notified not to return books and to keep away from the building and all fines were remitted. In the yard at the back of the Library a bonfire blazed day and night and in the early morning dead bodies were dumped there on the way to the Hospital. Once or twice a day an old negro drove up in a rickety cart and carried the bodies away to the graveyard. The old Loganian Library on Sixth St. which had recently been emptied of its books, was handed over to the City by the Directors and turned into a hostel for children whose parents had died or deserted them. For many months after the fever was gone, this hostel was the scene of tearful recognitions of lost children or fierce encounters between parents, seeking to establish a rival claim.

There is one episode in connection with the Yellow Fever for which the superstitious have sought a ghostly explanation. On the night of Sept. 5th, when the fever was at its height, Benjamin Poultney, a Director, arrived at the Library to attend the monthly meeting. There he waited for two hours, gazing at the bonfire in the yard outside, but not another Director came. Ere he left he signified both his presence and his displeasure in the *Minute Book* thus—"*At a Meeting of the Directors, September the Fifth, 1793—present, Benjamin Poultney, who, after waiting till Eight o'clock, retired!*" The mark of exclamation is heavy, emphatic, a little sinister. On Oct. 3rd, there comes another entry in the same hand—"*The Directors being generally out of Town by reason of the prevailing Sickness were not notified to attend.*" Why, we cannot help asking, did Benjamin Poultney take the trouble to come to the Library that night and record in the *Minute Book* that he was out of town? The mystery deepens when we read in a printed

list of the victims of the Yellow Fever, dated twelve days *before*—
"*Sept. 21st, 1793. Died, Benjamin Poultney, merchant.*" A month
later the *Minutes* are resumed in the orderly hand of the Secretary,
Benjamin Morgan, but he has no observation to make upon the two
brief entries that had crept into the *Minute Book* since the last full
meeting of the Board.

There were later outbreaks of Yellow Fever, but none so fierce or
so dramatic as that which struck the city in 1793. The Library's
history resumes its normal tenor of tranquillity for many years after
that event. In 1824 the Marquis de Lafayette, on his journey through
America, was made an honorary member of the Library Company. He
returned thanks by sending a plaster bust of himself—not of Lafayette,
the dashing young cavalier of the American Wars, but Lafayette, the
obstinate yet disillusioned idealist of the French Revolution.

In 1808 the Pennsylvania Fire Company and later the Fame Hose
Company were allowed to erect their main buildings on the north-west
corner of the Library Yard. In 1831 the services of these two institutions were required for a fire that broke out in the Library. The
Directors were in the building at the time, enjoying their monthly
collation of oysters and fish-house punch. When the alarm of Fire!
rose from the street, one of their number opened a window and enquired
mildly of the crowd without where the fire might be. "Why, it's thee's
damned old library that's burning!" came the answer from the street.
The Directors descended in a body and led the charge of the fire-
brigade. Very few books were lost in the actual conflagration but a
portrait of James Logan and a bust of William Penn were destroyed.
For repainting largely from memory the vanished portrait of Logan
Thomas Sully was elected the sixth honorary member of the Library
Company—the other five being James Logan, John Bartram, George
Washington, John Adams and Lafayette. The fire, be it noted, broke
out in a grate recently placed in the Library with a view to making
the building more fire-proof. There was correspondence with the In-
surance Company, but no hearts were touched. The Fame Hose Company was also criticised for wielding its hose across the charging-desk
with more gusto than discretion. It was found almost impossible to
open many of the books that the Fire Brigade had saved and others
were ruined by mildew.

From 1785 to 1851 the Library was happy in the care of three Librarians of more than usual ability—Zachariah Poulson, George Campbell and John Jay Smith. Poulson was a man of abounding vitality

whose energies were not swallowed up by the Library. He was an enterprising newspaper editor and a philanthropist of wide sympathies. His tenure of office was marked by many changes and reforms, accompanied by frequent summons to a Special Meeting. Campbell was a scholar and a lover of music, John Jay Smith a botanist and a landscape gardener. It was through the efforts of these three men that the Library Company was built up into the great repository of *Americana* that it is to-day. John Jay Smith retired in 1851 to devote himself to writing, but he did not die until 1881. There are still men alive who remember "John Jay." He loved to tell the younger generation that when he first came to the Library as Librarian (in 1829) the older members would tell him how Dr. Franklin stood *thus* beside the latticed book-shelves in Carpenters' Hall, how General Washington came slowly *so* up the "new Library" steps and how Mr. Robert Morris always dropped books and papers behind him *thus* when he left the Library.

On March 19th, 1785, the Library Company purchased at a "public vendue" for the sum of 104 pounds, six shillings, many of the books, papers and sketches gathered together by Pierre-Eugene du Simitière for his "American Museum" in Philadelphia. Du Simitière may rightly claim the title of first collector of *Americana*. He was born in Geneva. By profession he was a painter of miniatures, by choice a naturalist, but long life in a young country turned him into an antiquary. By 1750 he had found his way by a route uncharted and for reasons unknown to the West Indies and for ten years wandered round the islands, collecting botanical specimens, beetles, butterflies, sea-stars and other mild curiosities. In 1764 he settled for a short while in New York and rummaged industriously among the old Dutch archives. By 1766 he had set up house in Philadelphia and there spent the rest of his life. He drew portraits, designed medals, served the American Philosophical Society as curator and, with the advent of the Stamp Act and the Revolution, went on collecting material for the study of American history with increasing ardor. Among his well-wishers in his historical enterprises were General Steuben and Benedict Arnold, George Washington—who sat to him for a portrait —and John Adams—who found him "a very curious man." Finally in 1782 he opened his collections to public view under the name of *"The American Museum"* in his own house. He died on Oct. 22nd, 1784, and lies buried in a nameless grave in St. Peter's churchyard.

Du Simitière's main collections were bound in ten volumes. He had a method in his collecting, but from time to time his perspective changed. The first volume contains his observations on the fauna and flora of Jamaica, San Domingo and other West Indian islands. In New York his interest turned towards early Colonial history— Dutch and English. He gathered together a great deal of first-hand information about the trial and execution of the Dutch Governor, Jacob Leisler, in 1691, as well as many pamphlets, printed by Zenger and others, at the time of the famous Zenger trial. Later his fancy ran to Indians—a race whom he held to be doomed to extinction by the white man. He built up a magnificent collection of Indian Treaties (1721–1736) in printed form and manuscript, together with many letters from Conrad Weiser, giving an account of his wanderings among Indian tribes. Another volume contains the story of du Simitière's own voyage to Canada in 1775, to which are added notes taken down from the lips of the trappers who were then first breaking into the yet unexplored wilderness of the Middle West. Over and above these treasures there was a manuscript account of Pennsylvania in 1753 by Samuel Evans, the architect's drawings for Harvard Hall (1764), the manuscript poems of John Maylem, an early New England poet, and, strangest inclusion of all, a correspondence on matters of literature with Tobias Smollett, the novelist. One of the most tantalising things about the whole collection is that du Simitière—most truthful of men—perpetually refers to records now completely lost as the source of his information. Sometimes he notes a book printed in America that survives to-day nowhere— neither in bibliographies nor on the book-shelves of any library. One amongst the books that came to the Library from his American Museum was printed in French. It is obviously of American manufacture. It has no title-page, but on the blank-space where the title ought to be du Simitière has written *Invitation aux Habitants des Illinois*, with the place of imprint underneath—Philadelphia, 1774. This is the first account printed in America of the Middle West. Its author is not known. The book has been ascribed to a certain François de Rastel, Chevalier de Rocheblave, military commandment among the Indians of the Illinois territory. There is no other copy known in the whole wide world. Du Simitière is our sole authority for saying that it was printed in Philadelphia.

In February, 1792, the Library Company was made trustee for the Loganian Library. This was the collection of rare and valuable books amassed by James Logan and intended by him to form the nucleus of a public library for the city. Logan had collected together over two thousand volumes. His son, Dr. William Logan, had added about thirteen hundred more. But the story of the Loganian Library must be told apart.

In March of 1799 a tall, handsome gentleman of distinguished manners and military bearing called at the Library. He announced himself as Mr. Henry Cox "of the Kingdom of Ireland." He was, he said, but recently arrived in America and wished to deposit with the Library Company certain papers and documents of value that he had received by inheritance from a grandfather. These documents were all together in a black box with a brief inventory enclosed. Their subject matter, it seemed, was Irish history in the reigns of Queen Elizabeth and the Stuart kings. The Library Company duly accepted the charge and the black box was laid away on a shelf.

Mr. Cox thereafter vanished from Philadelphia, taking with him a wife and children. He made his way to York, Pa., and there presented himself to the local Friends' Meeting with a letter of introduction from the Friends in Dublin. He was accepted into the fold and assumed the decent habiliments of a Quaker. Later he purchased a farm and set his whole family to work upon it. Neighbouring farmers watched his efforts at first with sardonic amusement. It was plain that neither he nor his family knew much about farming. Yet, as the years went by, they had to admit that the Coxes were quick at learning. The farm prospered and in time Mr. Cox moved to a larger property near Londongrove in Chester County. He took an active part in Quaker meeting, sometimes preaching but without great success. His talents ran more to worldly affairs, and his advice—always delivered with an air of authority—was much valued at the business meetings of the Friends. He was punctual in his attendance at all religious meetings, driving up to the meeting-house in a farm-cart and dumping all his children, as an onlooker put it, "like a load of potatoes" at the door.

Yet, despite his activity in Quaker affairs, there was whispering about Henry Cox among the Friends. He wore his Quaker costume, they said, as though it were military undress. Chance visitors to his house found musical instruments there and books of an unfamiliar tone of thought. His wife and daughters had a certain elegance of manner and speech which smacked of "other world's folk" and of an old world at that. And last of all, on more than one occasion Mr. Cox had in a fit of abstraction addressed the assembled Friends as "My

Lords." So, for a multitude of reasons, Henry Cox was known as "the Strange Friend."

Then suddenly in 1817 Friend Cox sold his farm in Chester County and with his whole family returned to Ireland. The next that his neighbours heard of him was that he had returned to the Anglican fold and had published a volume of verse, entitled *Metrical Sketches. By a Citizen of the World*—a copy was presented to the Library Company. His farming exploits were celebrated in a poem called *Pennsylvania Georgics*. It contains a fine apostrophe to clover—"Best plant, tho' latest known, Columbia's pride . . . Fruitful of hay or nurse of golden ears."

The mysterious Mr. Cox has provided Bayard Taylor with a short story—*The Strange Friend*. In sober fact he was the descendant of a former Lord Chancellor of Ireland. His birth name had been Hamilton, but he had taken the name of Cox on inheriting the estate of Dunmanway in County Cork from an uncle. He had served in the British Army in India and then, on returning to Ireland to take up his inheritance, found the estate overloaded with debt. He therefore left it in charge of a faithful steward and migrated with his whole family to America. So soon as he received word—after eighteen years of waiting —that his estate was freed of all encumbrances and that he could live upon it as a self-respecting landlord once more, he had packed up his traps and gone home again—as unobtrusively as he had come to Philadelphia.

Henry Cox either forgot his black box at the Library or made the Company a present of it. For close on forty years it lay unopened in its corner and accumulated dust and cobwebs. Then one day the Librarian—Mr. John Jay Smith—opened it and took stock of its contents. It was indeed a collection of documents of great value and interest, all concerned with the troubled history of Ireland from the reign of Queen Elizabeth to the reign of James II. There were letters signed with the autograph of Queen Elizabeth, with the sign manual of James I and James II, addresses from the Privy Council, correspondence of Lord Deputies, cardinals, statesmen, the manuscript memoirs of the Jacobite Marquis of Clanricarde, and so forth and so on. At once the Librarian had this treasure trove of historic matter bound and catalogued and for many years to come individual documents from the collection were proudly placed on display.

In 1866 a visiting English scholar was shown these documents. After due scrutiny he discovered that they were papers missing from the government archives of Ireland since 1690. How they had been purloined and how descended into the keeping of the Cox family remains a mystery. So far as Friend Cox is concerned, he had come by the black box innocently enough—as a heritage. Probably he had never studied the papers in great detail himself. But when he sailed from Ireland he had felt that this mysterious legacy from the past must not be left behind to fall into the hands of His Majesty's government. So he had brought the black box to America and stowed it away among the Library Company's books. It had not been so safe there as it ought to have been for, when the Librarian at last opened it, he found that unknown hands had been there before him and some of the papers were disfigured and others gone. Unfortunately for the Library's rights of possession in the remnant Henry Cox had made no reservation or trust about their safe-keeping. There was nothing, therefore, for the Library Company to do but to return the manuscripts to the Master of the Rolls in England. An offer to that effect was transmitted by the Directors to the Lords of the Treasury and was by them gratefully received.

Two good things emerged out of this romantic story. In 1897 the manuscript volume, known as the "Log of the Mayflower," was discovered in the Bishop of London's library in England. Under decision of the Court of Consistory in London it was returned to this country. "The precedent of the Library Company of Philadelphia (in returning the Henry Cox papers) has unquestionably played a considerable part in determining the action of the Court," said the London *Times* of March 26th, 1897. This was a return of courtesy for which all America may be grateful. But to the Library Company in particular the British Government made return by depositing with it as a free gift the Master of the Rolls Series, the Calendar of State Papers, the Historical Manuscripts Collection and other publications of a legal and historical nature.

In 1804 the Library received the legacy of a valuable collection of books from the Rev. Samuel Preston, D.D., Rector of Chevening in Kent, England. Dr. Preston's portrait—painted by Benjamin West—hangs in the Library—a typical John Bull Englishman in a parson's wig. After the peace had been signed in 1783 he had written to the Directors, congratulating them on the exploits of their fellow citizens and wishing the Library well in its new days to come. Benjamin West prevailed upon him to leave all his books to the Library Company when he died. Dr. Preston's reading was wide and his love of a good book catholic. Many valuable books came to the Library by his bequest. Most interesting among them, perhaps, is a metrical paraphrase of the *Psalms* and the *Book of Job*, published by George Sandys in London in 1638. Sandys, a former treasurer of the Virginia Company, is claimed as the first poet living on American soil to write a poem in the English tongue. During his sojourn of ten years on his plantation in Virginia (1621–31) he consoled himself for quarrels with his neighbours by translating the *Metamorphoses* of Ovid into English verse. The poem was published in London in 1626. A second edition (also in Dr. Preston's library) was published in 1632 in sumptuous folio form with curious and truly Ovidian illustrations by Solomon Savery. Sandys was criticised by some for bringing out a book of such erotic tendency as the *Metamorphoses*. He did penance by turning the *Psalms* and the *Book of Job* into English verse, getting Milton's friend and composer, Henry Lawes, to illustrate the text with musical scores. In his preface Sandys, a little smugly, patted himself on the back for not having translated that amorous book in the Bible, commonly called the *Song of Solomon*. The copy of this *Paraphrase of the Psalms* which came to the Library Company from Dr. Preston was originally presented by Sandys himself to the Earl of Arundel. Bound up in the volume are several manuscript poems signed with the initials G. S. (George Sandys). Among them is—need we say it?—a translation of the *Song of Solomon*. Sandys had been unable to resist the appeal of that book. He suffuses his translation in the proper Ovidian spirit. It is a lyrical drama—a series of passionate *arias* between a lover and his lass on their wedding night with a kindly chorus in attendance. These poems, perhaps, are the only manuscript poems in this country of George Sandys—the first English-speaking poet of America.

In 1812 James Cox offered his books—5000 in number—to the Library Company in return for a pension of $400 a year. The offer was accepted. Cox's portrait—painted, perhaps, by himself—followed the books. He was, to judge by the painting, a gentleman of sinister aspect with a portentous Roman nose. Like the other benefactor of the same family name, James Cox had a romantic career. He had emigrated from England as a very young man and had earned his living in Philadelphia as a painter and drawing master. Among his patrons had been two members of the Library Company—George Washington and Robert Morris. One day in his early manhood as he was walking down Almond St. he observed a charming lady stand-

WILLIAM MACKENZIE

From the portrait by John Naegle. In his hands he holds his *Golden Legend*—the first
Caxton to come to America—which he later presented to the Loganian Library.

ing on the steps before her front door. He recognised her as having come from his own village in England. They struck up a friendship there and then, and when in due course the lady died she made James Cox her heir. With a house and fortune now at his command Cox abandoned himself to book-collecting. His purchases at one bookstore alone in the city amounted to $1000 a year and he bought books avidly from England where he kept a shrewd eye on modern ventures in poetry and art. As time went by and he grew old, he became careless. His books were piled in heaps upon the floor of a second-story room in his house. There dust and cobwebs gathered over them and rats made merry with the covers. Gradually his friends died and were buried and at eighty Cox was left a solitary old man of eccentric habits. He had only two companions—a dog and a macaw. The dog accompanied him on his walks abroad and guarded his door, when he was at home, with grim snappings and growls. The macaw presided within doors—talkative and splendid of plumage, with a propensity to play malicious practical jokes on the few visitors to the house.

A member of the Library Company who had ventured to call on James Cox, finding him grown old and morose, persuaded him to gather up his books from the floor and give them to the Library Company. After some argument Cox agreed, on condition that he receive a pension to enable him to buy yet more books. The Directors took him at his word and old James Cox then handed over to them all his much-loved books. Within two years of receiving his pension he died, leaving yet more books to the Library. It was felt by some that this necromantic old man had found the Directors easy game. Yet who shall judge? Among the books of James Cox were many both interesting and curious, showing an original and imaginative kink in their owner. In particular did he love books about flowers and gardens and romantic landscape. Next in his favor came works of humor and fantasy, such as the writings of the youthful Washington Irving, and then the poets—the young poets of the day. One book among his stores of poetry was a slim volume of 121 pages bound in pale green boards—*Poems* by John Keats, pr. London by C. & J. Ollier, 3 Welbeck Street, Cavendish Square, 1817. Inside the front cover is still pasted the label of T. Muncaster, of 26 Church St., Liverpool, the bookseller's shop where some emigrant bought the book to beguile his voyage out to America. This nameless first owner parted with the book soon after he had landed, for James Cox bought it for two dollars in some book-barrow in Philadelphia, and may thus rank as the first resident of America to appreciate the poetry of Keats.

Not all the books came by bequest. Individuals made gifts of their own works. Hugh Henry Brackenridge presented his picaresque romance of frontier life in America, *Modern Chivalry* (1792 etc.)— perhaps the first American novel, if the business of a novel be to tell a story sometimes for its own sake, with a little talent for character-drawing and some desire to entertain, and not to lecture the young female in a series of spasmodic letters on the dangers of seduction. Charles Brockden Brown (a surer claimant for the title of first American writer of novels) presented his novels when they were first published—*Wieland* (1798), *Ormond* (1799), *Edgar Huntly* (1799), *Clara Howard* (1801). A gift more tragic in its circumstances came from John Fitch, the inventor of the steamboat. Discouraged by failure to obtain any backing for his invention in America he made up his mind to sail for France. Before sailing he sealed up the manuscript of his *Autobiography* and deposited it with the Library Company. The news from France in the year 1792 was not reassuring and he had fears that he might not return alive. He therefore left instructions that the seals of his *Autobiography* were to be broken one year after his death, the volume read and, if possible, published without fear of what he had said about persons in authority—as his only legacy to posterity and his own children. In France he fared no more happily than in America. Paris was wracked and torn with revolution, the guillotine was claiming more and more victims every month and no man had the heart or time to listen to Fitch on his invention of the steamboat. His funds gradually vanished and he shipped home as a sailor before the mast. He never came back to retrieve his manuscript. Ill and desperate, he drifted away into Kentucky and there killed himself.

Among those who knew John Fitch and thought but little of his invention was Jean-Pierre Brissot, known to French history as Brissot de Warville. He was the first of a long line of brilliant Frenchmen who were accorded the privileges of the Library—Volney, Talleyrand, du Pont de Nemours, Moreau de St. Mèry—and repaid its hospitality by the gift of books. Brissot, after imprisonment in the Bastille, had fled to London and thence came to Philadelphia in 1788 to study the question of the emancipation of the negroes, for in those early days he was famous as *"l'Ami des Noirs."* Foremost among the friends of the negro in America had been Anthony Benezet, a former native of France. Benezet had been a member of the Library Company and through his nephew, Philip, Brissot was allowed the freedom of its books. Ever voluble and impressionable, Brissot was charmed with the Quaker simplicity of Philadelphia and dashed into fray with the Marquis de Chastellux, a superior French nobleman who had deplored, somewhat splenetically, the absence of "the graces" in Philadelphia. Into the midst of his pleasant bustle in the Quaker city came the first low thunders of the French Revolution and Brissot hurried back to take up his share of the burden in ushering Republican virtue into France. He arrived in time to witness the downfall of the Bastille and to receive its keys from the insurgents as one of its most recent and distinguished victims. Thereafter he moved volubly and busily in the very heart of the Revolution, writing, expounding and even taking a turn at forming ministries. But not all the uproar of revolution made him forget the Library Company. As fast as he wrote a book or published a pamphlet he sent it post-haste across the ocean with his compliments to the Library. In the end he earned the fatal animosity of Robespierre and was guillotined with the Girondins on October 31st, 1793.

Moreau de St. Mèry was born in the island of Martinique. When the Bastille fell he was in Paris, taking an active part in the early struggles of the Revolution as the champion of the French colonies in the West Indies. At one time he had been veritable "king in Paris," when he had presided over the meetings of the Assembly, and the rightful King—Louis XVI—had been obliged to come before him as a humble suppliant. But with the later and more violent developments of the Revolution he had no sympathy and he had rapidly declined into obscurity. Unimportant though he was, he had, like Brissot, enlisted the malevolent notice of Robespierre but, more wisely than Brissot, he fled to America. In his *Voyage aux Etats Unis*, Moreau describes his first arrival in Philadelphia on the morning of May 21st, 1794. He came by packet-boat from Newcastle and as the city rose into view from the river with Christ Church steeple soaring above its chimney smoke, the effect, he says, was both "interesting and important." A nearer view, however, of its wharves and warehouses convinced him that "cupidity had presided over their construction." After a visit to Congress he was walking down Chestnut St. on his way to the Library when a stage-coach drove by. Someone waved excitedly to him from the roof and a moment later the coach drew up. Out of it limped a well-dressed gentleman and in another moment Moreau was smothered in the arms of Talleyrand, *çi-devant* Bishop of Autun. Away went the two friends in search of their compatriots in the city and *"qu'on pense s'il fut question de la Fayette!"* writes Moreau—Lafayette was not loved by these exiles from revolution.

Moreau set up shop as a bookseller at the corner of Front and Walnut Streets and there tried to interest Philadelphians in French literature. His shop became the rallying point of the French *emigrés* in the city—Talleyrand, Lameth, the Duc de Liancourt, Volney, Talon, Noailles. In the evenings, after the shop was closed, these exiles met in Moreau's parlor for a frugal supper of rice, milk and madeira, *"que Talleyrand fort aimait,"* and let themselves go gloriously on the great days of revolution in France and the beauty and amorous deficiencies of American women, until Mme. Moreau intervened and dragged her husband to bed. The bookshop was not a financial success. Philadelphians were keenly interested in the French Revolution, but they preferred to read about it in English translation. A few books Moreau sold to the Library Company (of which he gives a full description in his *Voyage*) but he gave them as a present yet more. He later returned to France to linger out his life in embittered obscurity.

Among Moreau's acquaintances in Philadelphia was an Englishman, William Cobbett, yeoman and radical and author of the *Rural Rides*. Like Moreau he was a political exile and like him he kept a bookshop. He translated Moreau's book on San Domingo and earned a sparse penny by teaching the French *emigrés* English. But this friendly relationship did not long endure. Though he might be a malcontent and rebel in England, Cobbett was a sturdy John Bull abroad. He found French political views popular in Philadelphia. His own people were insulted and derided in the newspapers. When Dr. Priestley, the English Jacobin, arrived in the city—smuggled out of his tyrant-ridden island in a beer-barrel, so the rumour went—he received a public reception. This was more than Cobbett could bear. "Hearing my country attacked on all sides," he writes, "I became her defender through thick and thin." He issued a pamphlet against Priestley and for the next five years (1795–1800) was immersed in political warfare—to his great joy, for Cobbett, who had soldiered once in Canada, loved a fight of all things. He published a newspaper —*Porcupine's Gazette*—and as "Peter Porcupine" became a power in American politics. No man was safe from his rugged assaults. The Spanish envoy was goaded into bringing a libel action against him. So, too, was Dr. Benjamin Rush, whom Cobbett had nicknamed "the great Sangrado" and ridiculed for his purging and bleeding during the yellow-fever outbreak. Dr. Rush was finally awarded $5000 damages, which Cobbett neither would nor could pay. He migrated to New York where he started another paper called the *Rush-light* in memory of his antagonist. But by now he was tired of newspaper wars in America. He returned to England, where for thirty years and more he fought in his own pugnacious way the causes of the poor and oppressed and was more than once charged with sedition. In 1817 he was back in America once more as a refugee, but this time he contented himself peaceably with farming until Queen Caroline's troubles found him back in England again. To-day Cobbett is remembered for his delightful "Rural Rides" over the English countryside in quest of the English people. He, too, may be enrolled in the fellowship of the Library Company, for he made full use of its books and throughout his turbulent career in Philadelphia saw to it that the Library was well supplied with the products of his pen.

This has been a long chronicle of the givers of books, but we cannot close without saying something about two characters who introduce an element of comedy into the tale—Lorenzo da Ponte, formerly of Venice and once an *abbé* of the Holy Catholic Church, and Joseph Woods, the "honest and diligent bookseller" of Billingsgate, London.

Mr. "de Ponty" and his wagon were a familiar sight along the pike roads of Pennsylvania between the years 1815 and 1818. Mr. "de Ponty" himself was a tall, high-shouldered gentleman with an oriental significance of nose and lean, toothless jaws forever wreathed in smiles. In manner he was vivacious, in speech voluble, particularly in objurgation and abuse. He gesticulated generously with his eyes, his eyebrows, his hands, his arms, and, at times, his legs. He seemed to be about fifty years old and spoke English, French, German and Italian with equal rapidity and unconcern. From his wagon he dispensed to inn-keepers and householders along the road familiar country produce mingled with such strange delights as maraschino, macaroni and rosolio (a concoction of his own). Often he would pause in his sales to recite whole stanzas from the works of Tasso and Metastasio or to tell *maintes plaisantes histoires* about his life in Europe—how he had spoken with emperors man to man and slept with mysterious princesses. Rumor had it that he was a kinsman of the French gentleman, Mr. du Pont, who owned the famous powder mills, but here the gossips were wrong. It was also said that in his tales of adventure in Europe Mr. "de Ponty" was a melodramatic liar. Engaging in narrative Mr. "de Ponty" could ever be, but a liar not always nor altogether. His ill-wishers—they consisted mainly of his own compatriots in America—roundly stated that he had been guilty of twelve distinct and different crimes in Europe, not excluding murder, incest and eating ham on Fridays.

This was Lorenzo da Ponte—priest, musician, gambler, poet, retail grocer, lover of the ladies, manager of theatres and distiller of wines and whiskey. Born at Ceneda on the mainland, he had spent his early manhood in Venice of the eighteenth century—in the land of Canaletto and perpetual sundown, of masks and carnival and gambling-hells, of wine and flowers and laughter in casinos and all the *plaisirs intimes*. For a time he had figured in the gay life of the city as an *abbé* with a reputation for wit and poetry. But this life closed when he was summarily banished by the Council of Ten. Lorenzo himself would have us believe that the pretext for his banishment was a sonnet and a trivial charge of sacrilege. The State Archives of Venice tell another story of a pretty young woman called Angioletta who eloped from her husband with the *abbé* in a gondola one night. Da Ponte discreetly removed himself from Venice before the sentence of banishment fell and made his way to Vienna, where the Emperor Joseph took a liking to him and made him librettist at the Imperial Opera House. He wrote the libretti for Mozart's operas—*The Marriage of Figaro, Don Giovanni* and *Cosi fan Tutte*. After numerous amours (so he tells us) with high-born ladies in darkened palaces and romantic beggar-girls beside the waters of Venice he had forsworn his orders and married a beautiful and cultivated English Jewess. On his honeymoon he stopped to see his former acquaintance Casanova, by now a disgruntled hermit living as librarian in the castle of Dux in Bohemia. With native tact da Ponte introduced his bride to the sulky old demirep as his most recent find in mistresses. Casanova later discovered the deception and, already a little jealous of da Ponte, forever afterwards wrote of him with virtuous derision. From Germany to Holland, from Holland to Paris and from Paris to London went da Ponte and his wife, their path forever dogged by police spies, constables and bailiffs. In London he embarked upon ambitious schemes of opera with John Taylor, but was forced to fly to escape arrest for debt.

By this time his wife's family, as cosmopolitan in their tastes as their vagabond relative, had wound up a career of more or less lucrative bankruptcies over the face of Europe and were spreading their

LIBRARY and SURGEONS HALL, in Fifth Street PHILADELPHIA.

Old Fifth Street Library

From the engraving by William Birch, 1799. This building, erected 1789–90, was the home of the Library Company until 1880. The statue of Franklin above the entrance and the iron balustrade of the steps still survive in the front of the Juniper-Locust St. building.

sails for America. Da Ponte accompanied them on their hopeful pilgrimage to a more innocent world. But in America at first he was (by his own account) as unfortunate as he had been in Europe. Brought over in a ship captained by "a scamp from Nantucket" (the words are da Ponte's) he had first gone into business in Elizabeth-Town with "a licentious wastrel" (again the words are da Ponte's). He moved thence to New York only to be arrested for debt by an Irish grocer. This wretch was some years later struck by lightning and killed in Savannah—a fact on which, says da Ponte with a smirk in his *Memoirs*, he has no comment to make. After much wandering he came to rest at Sunbury, Pa., and there set up a store for farm produce. God had made this part of the world a pleasant land of waterfalls and guelder-roses, but rightly, he declared, was the town named Sunbury, for there the sun indubitably was buried. The male citizens were mere "worms of iniquity," the women thieves and "Thaïses." His servants robbed him, his bookkeeper, "a seraphic Yankee," cheated him and finally his landlord, Tom Robins, commonly called "Big Tom Hundred Legs" from his ability to be in many places by day or night, sold him up. He was, da Ponte informs us, a man "sunk in filth and inured to every vice" and had earned the disapproval even of a people so lost in moral squalor as the natives of Sunbury.

Driven out of Sunbury in 1818 this ever-buoyant optimist made his way to Philadelphia and there stumbled on a new idea. He had called at the house of a young Italian who had recently arrived in the city, bringing with him a small library of "the sweetest flowers" of Italian poetry. Da Ponte kissed his fingers in an ecstasy and promptly conceived the plan of selling these books to the Directors of the Library Company—most of them were Quakers, he had been told, and so were men religious and little versed in Italian poetry or the wiles of a money-grubbing world. He bought the books from the young Italian, lodged them with a Frenchman and laid siege to the Directors. Dr. Philip Syng Physick he already knew—he had consulted him for a cracked rib and a broken collar-bone and had been cupped and placed on a diet of oysters and potatoes for his pains. Da Ponte did not like Dr. Physick—his manner was dry, his countenance "hypocritic" and he lacked social charm. With Mr. Zaccheus Collins he had more luck. The Library had no funds for the moment, he was told, but would gladly consider the offer. At the end of sixty days da Ponte went to the Library and was informed by "a certain not very courteous lawyer" that he might keep his books. At once a round of explosions followed. Da Ponte, we may be sure, shouted, shook his fist, wept, tore his hair and left in a rage. The Frenchman, with whom he had lodged his wares, overwhelmed him with abuse and sold the books to a bookseller. Da Ponte "sacrificed" the remnants of his business in Sunbury for $3000, burst in upon the startled bookseller and in a whirlwind of degrading epithets bought the books back. Then, with his "sweet flowers" of poetry round him in his own room once more, there came a pause for reflection—what, he asked himself in desperation, should he do now with these books? A still small voice suddenly whispered in his ear "Send them to New York!" "I took that word as an inspiration from Heaven," declares da Ponte. He sent his son with the books to New York and in three days the young man returned triumphant from the sale with money in his pocket.

This is da Ponte's account of his dealings with the Library Company. Like everything else that he tells us about his adventures it has a large element of truth and a strong dose of poetry in it. In sober fact he succeeded in selling a few books to the Library Company and as a token of his esteem gave them the text of his *libretti* for Mozart's operas. But he soon abandoned Philadelphia for "the noble, populous and beloved city of New York." There he prospered and was in due course appointed the first Professor of Italian History and Literature in the College of Columbia. He came back to Philadelphia once more in his later years—at the age of eighty-three—to launch an opera season at the Chestnut Street Theatre. The enterprise failed with unexceptional brilliance—thanks to the general rascality of human nature as displayed in Philadelphia. Before he died he wrote his fascinating and vivacious *Memoirs*, wherein he tells the story of his adventures with the Library Company with many other things, true and not quite true.

Joseph Woods, of Billingsgate, lacked (we suspect) the vagabond, voluble charm of da Ponte. So far as the Library Company is concerned, he lives only in the *Minute Books*. But his letters do not breathe the cheery confidence of Peter Collinson, who would wrap a dictionary in Bartram's breeches when he packed the Library Trunk, and allow no questions to be asked. Joseph Woods is anxious and apologetic, a little hesitant and even dubious now and then. It was this tone in his letters, perhaps, that made the Directors feel at times that his honesty was at fault. They had in 1783 commissioned him to spend what sums were left over from the purchase of the *Utile* upon a discreet purchase of the *Dulce*. Woods took advantage of this permission, but as time went on he grew more and more doubtful about his choice of books—some, he confessed in his letters, might be touched with "a novel tinge." And sometimes the Directors felt that way, too. Woods always pleaded the same excuse—his partner, Mr. Dillwyn, the literary member of the firm, was away from business, so he had been obliged to act upon his own poor responsibility. Mr. Dillwyn, it would appear, was always away from business. He was an invalid gentleman, who lived at Brighton-on-the-Sea, with an invalid wife and a large and growing family of invalid children. So, in default of his advice, more and more books "of a novel tinge" got packed into the Library Trunk.

It is to be feared that some of these books were remainders upon the shelves of Mr. Woods' shop or books that he had been unable to sell to anyone else. Along with works of solid information he packed such stuff as the *Lyrical Ballads* (1798) of Wordsworth and Coleridge into the Library Trunk—who wanted to read about wedding guests and "ancyent Marineres" or learn how to be haunted like a passion by a sounding cataract, when books of chemistry remained unread? or a novel, *Emma* (1816) by a lady unknown! or *Waverley* (1814) a novel by a gentleman unknown! or *The Antiquary* (1816) or *Rob Roy* (1817) by the unknown author of *Waverley*! or, to go back a few years again, a volume of *Poems* (1796) by an undergraduate of Jesus College, Cambridge, called Coleridge! or a foolish tale entitled *Rosamund Gray* (1798) by a fellow called Lamb! Frankly, Mr. Woods had no right to waste the Library's money on such literary trash. He had not even the excuse of knowing that he had sold to the Library Company for a few shillings in their very year of publication several "Firsts" that one day were to be worth hundreds of dollars—if the value of a poem may be appraised in dollars.

The Directors more than once complained to Mr. Woods (and later to his son) about his choice of books—without much lasting effect. Both *Waverley* and *Emma* were entered disgustedly in the stock catalogues as *Anon. Emma*, to say the least of it, arrived in Philadelphia in suspicious company—cheek by jowl in the same trunk with *Manfred*. The Shareholders no more, in most cases, than the Directors approved of Mr. Woods' choice of books—"O English Insipidity!" one has written in the margin of *Emma*. Scott, however, soon found favor and Byron went like hot cakes from the first. Coleridge's *Christabel* (1816) was not even finished in the shape in which Mr.

Woods had sent it. Nor did he ever take the trouble to furnish the sequel, so the shabby thing was bound up summarily with an odd set of pamphlets on silver currency and kindred subjects. Shelley, strange to say, fared a little better. A young lady (we guess) has written on the fly-leaf of the Library copy of *The Revolt of Islam* (*1818*)—

> This poet's verse melts on th' enraptured heart
> Til my every sense in extasy doth float.

Lorenzo da Ponte burst like Harlequin with his slapstick on the quiet air of the Library room. He brought with him the last enchantment of the eighteenth century, though, through no fault of his own, he left but little in the way of books behind him. Yet for that small service we must be grateful to him. And Joseph Woods of Billingsgate must be numbered, too, among the benefactors of the Library Company. For some troubled huckster's motive of his own he revealed to the eyes of its Shareholders a new world—he pushed open a magic casement for them, looking out upon the faery lands forlorn of English romance.

VI

BEFORE AND AFTER THE CIVIL WAR

I<small>N</small> the late thirties and in the forties Philadelphia woke up once
more from its provincial calm. Railroads and canals were bringing
new business to the town and its citizens throve and founded fortunes.
One sign of this revival was an outburst of journalism. Newspapers
sprang up on every side, magazines were started, died and rose again
and died. Matthew Carey, an exile from Ireland who had once worked
in Franklin's press at Passy, helped to found the publishing house of
Carey, Lea and Blanchard, and other publishing houses followed after.
Carey was a member and Director of the Library Company and a
generous benefactor with books. One of his hobbies was international
copyright. He cared not so much that English authors were pirated
in America, but he saw how hard it was for a native author to find a
market for his wares against the flood of cheap reprints of English
books. To his influence we owe, probably, the regulation passed by
the Directors that on no occasion should recent numbers of English
magazines or copies of recent English books be loaned, as once had
been the case, to publishers in the town or elsewhere. Such loans had
only too often served as the text for piracies.

With this new birth of journalism and publishing came a strange
literary underworld—designedly we call it underworld, for the staid
citizens of Philadelphia lived, for the most part, unconscious of its
existence. It numbered many writers of romance, many poets and
not a few half-wit geniuses—George Lippard, who wrote wild Gothic
romances and flamboyant novels about the sins of Philadelphia and
camped by night in a disused warehouse; Henry Hirst, who boated
restlessly on the Wissahickon, wrote a poem, *Endymion*, beautiful
by fits and starts, and died mad, thinking that he was the author of
The Raven. These forgotten authors poured their books in on the
Library and there are many *Lays* and *Twilights*, *Dreams* and *Reveries*,
mouldering unread to-day on its shelves. Only one of these volumes
of crepuscular verse has achieved anything like fame—*The Voices
of the Night*—and its author and donor, young Mr. Longfellow, did

55

not live in Philadelphia. When local talent failed that sleek remorseless anthologist, the Rev. Rufus Griswold, poured in his offerings. Truth to tell, Philadelphians gave their own authors small encouragement. They took their reading matter from New York and New England. Many "firsts" of Fenimore Cooper and Washington Irving still survive upon the Library shelves. Hawthorne from *The Scarlet Letter* (1850) onwards appears in numerous "firsts," and so, too, Longfellow from *Hiawatha* (1855) onwards. If the Library Company be any criterion, Herman Melville was widely read, for nearly all his "firsts" survive in duplicate. But, strangest survival of all in its original green boards, is Walt Whitman's *Leaves of Grass* (1855). Few people bought that book. Those to whom the author sent it as a gift usually burnt it. So far as record goes it was sent to the Library anonymously—could it have come as a gift from Walt Whitman himself? In any case the Library Company kept the book. What is more, they ordered nearly all Whitman's other works when they came out.

Only one great figure emerges out of Philadelphia's literary underworld of the forties—Edgar Allan Poe. Hither he came in search of work with the magazines in 1838, accompanied by his child-wife, Virginia, and the dauntless Mrs. Clemm, whose placid face, framed in a widow's bonnet, and ever empty basket were soon to become the terror of her neighbours. For close upon five years Poe worked and starved in Philadelphia and during that period he produced some of his finest work. Yet not much is really known of his life during those years. The biographers fill in the picture with tales of quarrels with editors, bouts of drinking, solitary wanderings and other gossip of old fogies after the event. The fact is that in Philadelphia Poe still lived in his friendless dreamworld and the only events of his life worth mentioning are his works—*The Tales of the Arabesque*, *The Gold Bug* and *The Raven*. There is a legend that he frequented the Library on Fifth St. Certainly his fellow-sailor on the Wissahickon and fellow-traveller towards madness and despair, Henry Hirst, was often there. But Poe, of the bleak, haunted eyes in his shabby military frock coat, was not allowed within the Holy of Holies where the members sat. He read without in the public room, where the Loganian Library was housed. In much of his writings of this period there are references to queer books of travel, above all to writers on the occult such as Agrippa and Glanville, whose works he could have found only on the shelves of the Loganian Library. Three of his books the Library Company bought—they may have bought more, but only these survive—*The Narrative of Arthur Gordon Pym* (1838), *Tales of the Arabesque and Grotesque* (1840) and his last work *Eureka* (1848). After his death Helen Whitman sent a copy of her memoir of the poet to the Library Company, perhaps because she had learnt from him how once he had worked and brooded among its books.

Philadelphia in those days was still a city that people dwelt in. The Library on Fifth St. was the centre of a social life of its own. On Sunday mornings there would be a cheerful gathering of beaver hats and sober bonnets on its steps when the churches and meeting-houses near-by disgorged their worshippers. On shopping days it was a favorite *rendezvous* for the old family carriage and the negro coachman. At all hours—particularly on hot summer days—school-boys came and went through its hospitable doors. These young gentlemen prowled along the book-shelves, climbed step-ladders, browsed on window-sills and generally extorted for themselves by dint of agility and craft privileges that had never been granted to the Shareholders. One of them, at any rate, Frank Stockton, repaid the debt that he owed to the books of the Library Company by becoming a writer of books on his own account. More than that, he expressed his gratitude in verse. It is a thought to play with—perhaps Edgar Allan Poe looked up from one of James Logan's books on the occult and his eyes fell in a dreamy stare upon a small boy squatting upon the bottom rung of a ladder, absorbed in the book upon his knees. That boy, too—had Poe known it—had a taste for the Arabesque and the Grotesque, but where Poe's fancy ran to sombre Houses of Usher or ghastly Masques of the Red Death, young Frank Stockton was even then filling his world with enigmatic Ladies and unaccountable Tigers and such delightful people as those two castaways of shipwreck, Mrs. Lecks and Mrs. Aleshine.

The true source of romance in any library is, after all, the wanderer who comes to its doors by chance. Washington Irving came to the Library Company for news of Major André, when he was writing his life of Washington. Edwin Forrest, the actor, read the newspapers in the outer room with an air of melancholy disdain. Thackeray spent only a few days in Philadelphia, but he left America with grateful memories of "the dear old Library" on Fifth St. Nor were these the only birds of passage in those years just before the Civil War. Few people in America to-day know much about Karl Almquist, the author of the *Briar Rose* romances. He is, however, a famous name in Swedish literature—an elusive, somewhat sinister character with the genius of a Byron and the ill-fame of a Eugene Aram. He fled from Sweden to escape trial on a charge of forgery and attempted murder and settled in Philadelphia at a house on Arch Street under the *alias* of Professor Louis Gustawi. As "Prof. Gustawi" he frequented the Library round-about the years 1855 to 1860. In thanks for courtesies received he now and then made presents of books to the Library. Among his gifts was a Swedish grammar with his own (real) name printed as author on the title-page. Eventually he left Philadelphia for Texas. Somewhat ungratefully, he carried off with him two books belonging to the Library Company—one was a Homer, the other his own gift, the Swedish grammar. After years of wandering he found his way back to Europe and died, still an exile, in Bremen. His family, very honestly, returned the long-lost Homer to the Library after his death, but the Swedish grammar was a rarity and that they kept for reasons of sentiment. Thus, unknown to itself, the Library Company had played host to—we must not say a murderer—but to a great writer of romance, another exile from a foreign land.

The Civil War came and went and left little outward mark on the life of the city or the Library Company. After the war the great social pilgrimage towards Paoli set in. Private houses slowly vanished from the neighbourhood of Fifth St. and left it a wilderness of banks and business houses. The time had now come to move westwards with the Shareholders. Possible sites were discussed round about Thirteenth St. and as early as 1856 a building fund was started by voluntary subscription from the Shareholders. Into the midst of these plans and deliberations a bomb fell whose detonations have not ceased to reverberate yet.

At a meeting of the Directors on June 3rd, 1869, Mr. Henry J. Williams, one of the Directors, laid upon the table a certified copy of the will of Dr. James Rush, lately deceased, wherein he left his private fortune of over a million dollars to the Library Company of Philadelphia under certain conditions. Mr. Williams requested his fellow Directors to take immediate steps to ascertain the decision of the Shareholders on accepting the bequest of Dr. Rush under the terms prescribed. The meeting broke up in some agitation and in the general confusion only lukewarm thanks were given to Mr. Williams for the news he had brought and but faint appreciation was expressed for the generosity of Dr. Rush.

The story that follows is a chapter of ineptitudes. Anyone who has toiled through the mass of correspondence and legal papers that have

PHOEBE ANN RIDGWAY

Mrs. James Rush, in whose memory the Ridgway
Branch was built. From a miniature.

DR. JAMES RUSH

Son of Benjamin Rush, the Signer, and founder of the
Ridgway Branch. From a miniature.

accumulated round Dr. Rush's will, cannot help exclaiming "Oh why did Franklin ever die!" If he had lived, some common sense and a great deal more good will would have been brought to bear upon the case. But before we say anything more about his legacy, let us speak of Dr. Rush and of his yet more famous wife, "Madam" Rush.

James Rush was the fourth son of Dr. Benjamin Rush, Signer of the Declaration of Independence and "the great Sangrado" of Cobbett's diatribes. With many amiable qualities he inherited from his stern and vigorous father the firm conviction that "everyone else are fools." He followed his father's calling and as a young man studied medicine abroad in Edinboro' and Germany. When he returned to Philadelphia he moved in society for a few years and acquired a reputation for charm and then at the age of twenty-seven married the great local heiress, Phoebe Ann Ridgway.

Phoebe Ann was of Quaker stock, the daughter of Jacob Ridgway, a shrewd manipulator of the foreign exchange who had long been the rival of Stephen Girard in wealth and commerce. Her father's affairs kept him for long periods abroad, at Antwerp and Paris, and in France Phoebe Ann spent much of her girlhood and youth. She had seen Napoleon and spoken with Mme. Récamier and Mme. de Staël. She came back to Philadelphia, determined to introduce the salon and other modes of French society into the social life of America. With her marriage to James Rush she embarked upon the career that made her uncrowned Queen of Philadelphia. Nature had done little to help "Madam" Rush, as she liked to be called. Her one physical charm was a bright and vivid complexion. Otherwise she was stout, with features strong and humorous rather than beautiful, and short of stature—"an empress," says one of her admirers, "in the body of a Dinah Shadd." In later days her stoutness grew to be a theme of merriment even to herself and her bright complexion settled into strawberry red. But she brought to her task a self-possession which no sneer could daunt, a wit which no rival could match and a temper which no enemy brooked a second time. Old Philadelphia denied her claims to supremacy—angrily and in vain. They bade her be content with native ways and more true to her Quaker breeding, and she laughed. They begged her husband to hold her in check, and he shrugged his shoulders. She bore down all opposition by sheer vigor, by a jovial humor that found expression in sharp phrases and devastating comments. Her sayings are still remembered. "Psha, Madam, 'tis the neat fabrication of a keen woman," she said, when some kind friend whispered in her ear the latest scandal, and "little dry despots of the parlour, little Napoleons of the hearth-rug" she called those ladies who insisted that morning calls be returned. In 1843 she built herself a magnificent house between Nineteenth and Twentieth Sts. on Chestnut St., commonly called "the Rush Palace." It was so designed that it could accommodate eight hundred guests at one time. It contained a long suite of reception rooms—the Armorial Room, the Crusaders' Gallery, the Marie-Antoinette Room, the Blue Chamber and the Damask Parlor. The furniture was splendid rather than elegant—buhl and ormolu, heavy crystal chandeliers, gold candelabra and miles on miles of landscapes of the Munich School. In these glorious rooms Mario and Grisi sang. Princes, poets and authors from all over the world thronged the inner sanctuary where Madam Rush sat enthroned and ablaze with diamonds—Joseph Bonaparte, Longfellow, Washington Irving, Charles Dickens. The Rush dinners at twenty-five tables loaded with gold plate were the most famous entertainments of their kind in the country. And the Rush Balls were the crown of a perfect season.

The times had changed since Logan's austere tranquillity or the stately Whig elegance of Washington's day. The age of millionaires and commerce was at hand and Madam Rush was its sturdy harbinger. She was greater than other tyrants of the social world in that she brought humor to her game and the democratic grand manner of a Duchess in a Balzac novel. Her foible was to startle and command and she took the whole world into her confidence. Nor were her social activities bounded by the walls of her "palace." "I cannot meet everyone that I wish in my house," she said, "it saves time to meet them on the street." Every morning in fine weather at the hour of noon she emerged from her palace, beribboned, beflounced and flanked to right and left by a brace of young cavaliers, and sailed down Chestnut St., like a stately steamboat on the Delaware with two tugs bobbing behind. As she sailed she smiled and dispensed favors and frowns, nodding upon this one, clasping hands with that one, dismissing another from her view and haughtily shielding her face behind a parasol from the gaze of the lowly and curious. A whisper and a flutter ran before her under the trees, half sardonic, half reverential, "Here comes Madam! make way for Madam Rush!" These promenades were as famous in their day, we are told, as those of Beau Brummel on the Mall in London, and woe betide any humbler favorite who absented himself too long from duty at the "Curbstone Court." One fine day in 1853 came her greatest triumph. All traffic

was halted, all voices were hushed, even the trees stood motionless
on Chestnut St., while Franklin Pierce, President of the United States
of America, bent, hat in hand, in deferential converse with "the
magnificent Madam Rush" on the sidewalk.

"You ought to be a happy man, Dr. Rush," said a lady once, a
little ironically, to the Doctor in his wife's gilded conservatory hung
with tropical flowers, where she had found him meditating alone.
"I thank you, Madam," said the doctor drily. "I have always been a
happy man." He had never shared his wife's social ambitions and
when dinners and balls filled his house with guests, he withdrew quietly
to his books. His ambitions were intellectual and his favorite studies
were music and psychology. He essayed authorship more than once.
His *Philosophy of the Human Voice* ran into several editions in an
age of oratory. His *magnum opus* was a learned work entitled *An
Analysis of the Human Intellect*—in two volumes—at once original,
atrabilious and verbose. He even essayed drama in a five-act tragedy
in blank verse—*Hamlet, a dramatic Prelude*—not to be confused with
a play of similar title by another author. The blank verse is involved
and splenetic. The hero is an obvious portrait of the author—a sour
idealist in a world of knaves and fools, who finds consolation only in
the society of hermits, clowns and such-like philosophers in tubs. There
is something rotten in the modern state, he feels, and the Doctor
turns aside in a footnote to pour down scorn upon Turkish baths.

Madam Rush died in October, 1857, under somewhat tragic circumstances at Saratoga Springs. Her husband was left in mournful possession of her fortune. He had long since become a recluse and found
his new wealth a burden and a bore. He lived for twelve years longer,
retired and solitary, among his books. The few people who knew him
describe him as being "strange and gentle," an unworldly, kindly,
somewhat taciturn old man with secret enthusiasms of his own—
for collecting *Poor Richard* almanacks, for the poetry and music of
the negro, for Napoleon's descent upon Egypt and books about
Egyptian antiquity, for Catherwood's colored lithographs of Yucatan,
for Holbein's drawings and Piranesi's engravings, for old song-books,
books of sport and books about Etruscan vases—in a word, for the
grandeur or the simplicity of past time and distant scene. But one
crochet overpowered all the rest—his profound pessimism, his dreary
contempt for every tendency of the age into which he had been born.
He died alone in his palace of buhl and ormolu in 1869—an atheist,
forbidding any service to be held over his bones.

His marriage with Phoebe Ann had been childless. Madam Rush —perhaps to please her "fond hermit," as she dubbed her book-loving husband—had expressed a wish that her money should one day go to the Library Company. Accordingly on February 26th, 1860, Dr. Rush made his will. A gentler will than this could not have been written. Briefly and concisely he left his wife's fortune and his own books in trust to the Library Company on condition that they erect a branch library in memory of his wife, to be called the Ridgway Branch of the Library Company of Philadelphia—his own name he wished to be entirely forgotten in the bequest. There were a few other conditions attached. No lectures were to be given in this library nor were any collections of pictures or statues to be formed for it. It was to be erected on a site between Fourth and Fifteenth Sts. and Spruce and Race Sts. —the very area, as it happened, in which the Directors were contemplating the erection of a new Library building.

Unfortunately during the next nine years Dr. Rush had more than one attack of codicils and the will grew from seven pages to thirty-one. With every page his vision of his library wavered and changed; sometimes it was a grandiose temple, at other times an austere hermitage. And the conditions and prohibitions grew from page to page. Dr. Rush was to be buried with his wife on the premises of the Ridgway Branch; the membership of the Library Company was to be restricted to its number at his death; the Ridgway funds were to be invested only in real estate, mortgages and state and government loans. In his last codicil but one Dr. Rush made speeches to posterity, airing his prejudices about "cushioned seats" and "lounging readers," "mind-tainting reviews," "scribblings of poetry and prose" and "those teachers of disjointed thinking, the daily newspapers." Unfortunately, by being incorporated in a will, these prejudices acquired the force of law, when Dr. Rush had merely intended them as an expression of personal opinion.

All this and more the Directors might have borne for the sake of a million dollars. But there was one last difficulty that lay beyond the will as it had been written. Mr. Williams, Dr. Rush's brother-in-law, had been appointed sole executor with full powers to purchase a site, erect the Ridgway building and in his discretion over-ride any clause in the will. This was the snag on which his fellow Directors struck. For Mr. Williams informed them that shortly before his death Dr. Rush had called him to his bedside. He was troubled about the site of his library. He questioned Mr. Williams about many possible sites and asked whether Broad St. were not the finest street in Phila-

RIDGWAY BRANCH

Exterior. Erected 1876–8 in memory of Phoebe Ann Ridgway—
"the magnificent Madam Rush."

delphia. Finally he had begged Mr. Williams to inspect a certain site on Broad St., and if it were suitable, to make arrangements for its purchase and to promise faithfully to build the library there and nowhere else. This purchase had been made, this promise had solemnly been given and Dr. Rush had died relieved and happy. The site chosen and already purchased at Dr. Rush's behest was on Broad St., between Christian and Carpenter Sts., and there, declared Mr. Williams, the Ridgway Branch was going to be built.

There followed nine years of acrimonious battle and dispute. The Directors felt that the site on Broad St. was too far from the centre of the city and that it would be better to adhere to the more central area mentioned in the will itself by Dr. Rush. Mr. Williams pointed out that he was empowered to over-ride that clause in his own discretion and, in any case, he felt himself bound by his promise to Dr. Rush. He demanded peremptorily that the Shareholders state whether they accepted or refused the bequest. The Directors, acting upon legal advice, replied that they were not called on in the name of the Library Company to accept or refuse until Mr. Williams had erected the Ridgway Branch and tendered a conveyance of the trust. Mr. Williams thereupon withdrew in anger from the Board and announced his intention of building the Ridgway Branch without further consultation with the Library Company. A Special Meeting of the Shareholders was called for June 29th (1869). The Directors laid their point of view before the meeting—that the time had not yet come either to accept or refuse the trust. There was prolonged discussion, several alternatives were proposed, but no decision was reached. Finally a committee of six Directors and six Shareholders was appointed to study the whole matter once more and report back to the Shareholders. On October 5th the meeting was summoned again to hear the Committee's report. Again there was prolonged discussion. The report, apparently, had only added to the general doubt and dissension. It made five recommendations, the first of which entailed immediate acceptance of Dr. Rush's legacy according to the terms prescribed. It was finally decided that a stock-vote should be taken from the Shareholders on October 19th, between the hours of ten and four, on this and the other resolutions.

On October 19th, 1869, the Shareholders gathered together to vote. The newspapers of the day give vivid and somewhat ironical accounts of the scene. The tellers sat, silent, white-haired, Rhadamanthine, at a table draped in the American flag under the darkened portrait of John Penn. Oliver Cromwell's clock ticked the slow minutes and from hour to hour the chimes and the bell from Independence Hall rang through the windows. The Shareholders were agitated and divided in counsel, "distracted between their natural love of gain and the menace of all their privileges and habitudes." On the steps outside there was a perpetual coming and going, a buzz of excited conversation and eager lobbying. Some members climbed the steps, stayed to talk and then went down again. Others pressed resolutely forward, disdaining counsel. An uneasy whispering filled the building within and eyes were cast in desperation at the colossal bust of Minerva in the gallery above the tellers' table, as if asking guidance from that quarter in this hour of mental trial. Shadows of autumn lengthened and deepened along the latticed bookshelves. One by one the Shareholders tottered up to the table and dropped their votes, folded suspiciously, into the urn, while the tellers still sat bland and inscrutable. At length the Cromwell clock struck four—a miracle, for sure, for it has never struck since! The whispering died down like a spent breeze. The votes were counted and re-counted in the gathering gloom. Of 969 members 378 had abstained from voting, 298 had voted for the immediate acceptance of Dr. Rush's legacy under the terms prescribed, and 293 against. The trust had been accepted. But a resolution involving an expression of gratitude from the Library Company to Dr. Rush for his munificent bequest had unfortunately been turned down by a majority of 25 votes, and sadly and confused the meeting dispersed.

This was surrender, but Mr. Williams steadfastly declined to be mollified by its terms. He insisted on building the Ridgway Branch on Broad St. and as the Directors still protested, refused to consult with the Committee that they had appointed to advise with him. The matter was carried to the courts. The Directors sought to inhibit Mr. Williams from building because by his promise to Dr. Rush on his death-bed he had precluded himself from using the full discretionary powers granted him by the will. This neat legal point was disputed from court to court. It was decided in every court in favor of the Library Company—except the last.

Henry J. Williams had won the last battle in a Civil War. Forthwith he called in an architect—Mr. Addison Hutton—and started building the Ridgway Branch on the site on Broad St. The building that arose there was a magnificent Doric temple, built of solid granite —one of the noblest buildings of its kind in any country. It was nearly four times the size of its parent building—the old library on Fifth St.—and $850,000 in all was spent upon its erection. But the squabbles were not yet over. Colonel Manners, a relative by marriage of Dr.

Rush, brought action against Mr. Williams as executor, and the Library Company as beneficiaries, of the will. Then, as the Library Company showed no signs of moving into the building, Mr. Williams entered suit to compel them to accept the trust. The Directors felt themselves bound by the vote of October, 1869, and accepted on May 6th, 1878. A day later Mr. Lloyd Smith, the Librarian, over a wilderness of deserted scaffolding, mounds of earth and craters full of water, made his entrance into the Ridgway Branch, carrying the chief treasure of the Library Company, Richard Frame's poem, *A Short Description of Pennsilvania* (Phila. 1692) in his hand. He found the interior unfurnished and bare and almost destitute of bookstacks. These had to be added later. Gradually during the next few years all the more valuable books of the Library Company were moved to the fire-proof Ridgway Branch. To-day it houses one of the most valuable collections of *Americana* in the world.

The Ridgway Branch long suffered for the confusion and cross purpose that attended on its birth. A wag—for the first time in 1879 —described the building as a "tomb," a "mausoleum," a "morgue," because the man who gave the money for it lay buried in its vaults. The joke flourished for fifty years, unabated and unchanged. Age, apparently, could not wither nor custom stale its infinite variety. Fantastic legends were told of Dr. Rush's will. He had expressed a pious hope that only "the best names in fiction" would be permanently lodged in his library. From that it was quick work to say that the doors of the Ridgway Branch were closed to *all* fiction. The general opprobrium spread to all the collections of the Library Company housed there. Books that had rightly been a source of pride to the City so long as they were housed in the Old Fifth St. Library were dismissed in sober accounts of Philadelphia as dreary trash, because they were in the Ridgway Branch. But later generations are not concerned with that reverend squabble of seventy years ago. Though it may be situated somewhat off the beaten track the Ridgway Branch is known to-day the whole country over as one of the great libraries of *Americana*. Men come there from far in search of books and knowledge that can be found in no other library in the world. And for long the Ridgway Trust has contributed generously to the support of the Library Company and of its other building on Juniper St. Only a disastrous slump in its income from real estate during the past few years has prevented it from continuing that support. To-day the Library Company without fear counts among its benefactors the kindly and eccentric James Rush.

VII

WITH the acceptance of the Ridgway Trust the history of the Library Company grows quiet again. Not a very large sum came into its care from Dr. Rush's estate after all the expenses of erecting the Ridgway Branch had been paid, but under the careful nursing of the Treasurer, Mr. George Maurice Abbot, the fund was increased and became a valuable asset to the Library Company.

It was decided to go on with the scheme for erecting a new main building for the Library further west than Fifth St. One of the Directors, Mr. Joseph Fisher, left by bequest $50,000 for that purpose. Accordingly in 1880 the present site at Juniper on Locust St. was purchased for $60,000. At that time this site was known commonly as "the Village." It consisted of a group of little old red-brick houses, built round a green or yard which, it is said, was an Indian reserve, dating from William Penn's days. Of these old houses the Centaur Bookshop is the only survival to-day. As far as possible it was hoped that the old Fifth St. building would be reproduced in the new building. The architect chosen for the task was Mr. Frank Furness, a man of great originality in design. In so far as Victorian red-brick Gothic can faithfully reproduce the Georgian classic style, the present main-building of the Library Company is, perhaps, an adequate replica of the old Fifth St. Library. The statue of Franklin, his memorial stone and the double flight of steps with the iron balustrade were removed from the old building to the new. The statue now stands above the main-entrance door and there is a legend that every night it descends from its niche, walks round the Library and then sits on a fire-plug and drinks a mug of beer. Within a short time the new building was found too small. Again a Director came to the rescue. Henry Charles Lea presented $50,000 to the Company and the rear portion of the present building, called Lea Hall in his honor, was built in 1889.

The old Library on Fifth St. was taken over by a bank and eventually destroyed.

In every building it ever owned the Library Company has had its tutelary ghosts. Franklin's statue walked the old Library on Fifth St. and still walks its new home at Juniper on Locust St. It is a matter of recorded fact that a caretaker's child was wandering round the stacks at the Ridgway Branch one evening when she was met by a ghostly gentleman in powdered wig and knee-breeches who rapped her so hard with his cane that she had to be removed to hospital. Perhaps we may add the ghost of Walt Whitman to this select company. There are still those alive who remember him in the flesh, pacing restlessly round the outer room of the Juniper-Locust building, a wide hat on his head and his beard stained with tobacco-juice. It would be pleasant to believe that "the good grey poet," now that he is dead and famous, joins Poor Richard for a nightly drink at the fire-plug.

A ghost that is never laid in a modern library is the catalogue. In the eighteenth century cataloguing had been a simple affair. Human knowledge could be docketed under a few headings such as History, Philosophy, the Greek and Latin Classics, and there was little difficulty about arranging and classifying books. They were lifted from the Library Trunk, arranged by folio, quarto, octavo, duodecimo, and numbered progressively under each size, with Sacred Letters taking precedence of all profane letters. They were then entered by size and number in the stock catalogue and finally placed on the shelves, grouped by size first and subject matter after. From time to time printed catalogues were issued (1733, 1741, 1757, 1764, 1772, 1789). In the earlier catalogues size was the only classification recognised, but in 1789 the titles were grouped under subject headings, with Sacred Letters still in the place of honor. In 1807 a more ambitious catalogue was issued. The books were listed twice over, by subject and by size, with numbers marked against each title and an index of authors at the end.

The last printed catalogue appeared in 1856. Thereafter we note the birth-pangs and infantile diseases of the modern card-index system. In 1857 the Librarian, Mr. Lloyd Smith, a man of commendable ingenuity, inaugurated a system known as "current cataloguing." From that year onwards the titles of all books were entered, with their size and number, under the author's name on stiff, six-inch cards, which were then filed away alphabetically in sliding wooden drawers. The system was by no means perfect. Besides author heading there were title-headings and subject-headings but under title and subject the seeker after knowledge received no other information than

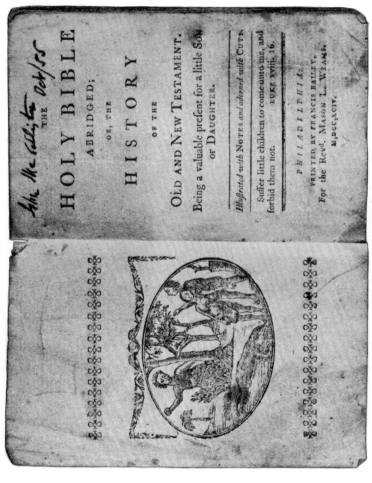

A CHILDREN'S BIBLE, WITH WOOD-CUTS

Pr. Philadelphia, 1794. This extremely rare little volume was compiled by Parson Weams, the author of *The Life of Washington*.

the name of author—a trick which has kept men running desperately backwards and forwards the whole length of the catalogue ever since. Somewhere about 1876, Mr. Lloyd Smith embarked upon further schemes of reclassifying the books of the Library Company by subject under alphabetical symbols. He still clung to the old classification by size, but neglected to classify under author—an omission which has led to long pilgrimages round the stacks in search of the works of a single author. This reform was slow in getting under way. It was introduced into the Ridgway Branch in 1878, into the Juniper-Locust building in 1889. It was unfortunately not incorporated in the card-catalogue until 1893. There were many causes for this delay. A first cause was that the books themselves were under annual sentence of expulsion from the Old Fifth St. building. Then when that move was made, one-half of the books migrated to the Ridgway Branch and the other half to the building on Juniper and Locust Sts. And finally Mr. Lloyd Smith died. His experiments in cataloguing were not altogether successful—it would be fairer to say that they were frustrated by circumstances over which he had no control—but we note them as a first essay in the modern science of cataloguing.

Among the Directors we still note distinguished names—Dr. Weir S. Mitchell, the physician, Henry Charles Lea, the historian, Horace Howard Furness, the Shakespearean scholar—if we may mention a few names from the not so distant past. Lloyd Smith had succeeded his father, John Jay, in 1851, as Librarian. He in turn was succeeded in 1887 by J. G. Barnwell. In 1907 George Maurice Abbot, who had been Treasurer since 1886, succeeded as Librarian. Mr. Abbot had been in the service of the Library ever since he was a boy of seventeen. He had come there on June 24th, 1863, a week before the Battle of Gettysburg, and during Mr. Lloyd Smith's absence on duty at the war, he was left in charge of the Library on Fifth St.—most unwillingly, as his great desire was to serve in the war. His appointment as Librarian was a well deserved recognition of his long and arduous labors for the Library Company. He celebrated his fiftieth year of service in 1913 by publishing a short history of the Library to which this present account is greatly indebted. He retired from duty in 1929 after sixty-six years of single-minded labour on behalf of the Library Company. He died on October 13th, 1934. In the long list of Librarians he will ever be remembered with affection and esteem.

In 1881 John A. Macalister presented a large collection of material relating to the Civil War—including broadsides, political caricatures and old marching songs—and a second collection of pictures and engravings of old Philadelphia buildings, old play bills, etc. He also presented several books amongst which was a small Children's Bible illustrated with wood-cuts, printed in 1794 for Parson Weams, the biographer of George Washington, and by him peddled around the country. This is a volume so rare that, it is said, only one other copy exists.

The benefactions of books continued. In 1904 Mr. Charles Sower, descendant of Cristoph Saur, the first German printer in America, presented, perhaps, the most complete collection of Saur imprints in this country, starting with the *Zionitischer Weihrauchs Hugel* (1739) and coming down through all the ramifications of the Saur family to the mid-nineteenth century.

On April 21st, 1932, the Library Company celebrated the Two Hundredth Anniversary of its foundation, a ceremony to which came distinguished visitors from all over the country. In the outer room of the Library there was a display of over a hundred of the more valuable books in our possession—medieval illuminated books of hours, Caxton's *Golden Legend*, numerous Franklin imprints, *Americana* of great rarity dating from 1532, early plays and play bills, and first editions from Donne to Keats and Shelley and from William Penn to Walt Whitman. The leading addresses were made by Mr. Owen Wister, President of the Board of Directors, and Miss Agnes Repplier, to-day our only Honorary Member.

With this—the Two Hundredth Anniversary of the Library's foundation—we will close our story—for the moment only. During the past four years the Library Company has endured poverty and hardship in common with the rest of the world. But it moves onwards to its next hundred years of life in the spirit of its founder—with Cheerfulness and Youth.

JAMES LOGAN

Founder of the Loganian Library. From a copy made by Thomas Sully from memory
of a portrait in the Library destroyed by fire, 1831.

THE LOGANIAN LIBRARY

formed by JAMES LOGAN, *1699-1751*

and incorporated with the Library Company, 1792

By AUSTIN K. GRAY
Librarian

JAMES LOGAN, the founder of the Loganian Library, was without doubt the most remarkable man residing in the American Colonies in the first half of the eighteenth century. He was born at Lurgan in the north of Ireland of a good Scotch family. His father was a school-master who had a strong scholarly bent. By the time that he was six-teen James had taught himself four languages—Latin, Greek, Hebrew and French. His knowledge of Latin was so thorough that he wrote in it with the same ease and correctness that he wrote in English. In later years he added Spanish and Italian to his accomplishments. The troubles of civil war drove his family from Ireland to England about 1690. They first settled in London and thence moved to Bristol. For a time James was apprenticed to a linen-draper. Later he assisted his father as a school-master. Finally he entered a mercantile house in Bristol as a clerk. All this time he continued to educate himself. His two chief hobbies were by now mathematics and its daughter science, astronomy. But natural philosophy, as physics were then called, chemistry and botany also attracted his restless and inquiring mind. By the time he was twenty-two he had amassed for himself a library of eight hundred volumes along the lines of his favorite studies.

His younger brother, William, settled in Bristol, became a dis-tinguished physician and was a great supporter of the Bristol Public Library, one of the earliest institutions of its kind in England. But James was destined for a wider sphere of activity. Tall, handsome, intelligent, masterful, he attracted the notice of William Penn, who invited him to come out with him on his last voyage to Pennsylvania (1699) as his secretary and confidential agent. Young Logan accepted and sailed with Penn on the good ship *Canterbury*. There is a tale told of this voyage. In mid-ocean a strange vessel was sighted. It was feared that it might be a pirate vessel. Penn retired below deck to pray, but Logan stayed above and with the captain made prepara-tions for a fight. The strange vessel—pirate or not—veered away and Penn came on deck again. He expostulated with his young secretary for his readiness to shed blood, but Logan retorted in some bewilder-ment "If thee didn't want me to fight, why didn't thee order me below?" This story is told in many versions; Franklin quotes it in his *Autobiography* as coming from Logan's own lips. But, apart from

all considerations of fairness to William Penn, it illustrates one quality
in James Logan that friend and foe alike confessed—his physical
courage.

For over fifty years he lived and labored in Pennsylvania. He held
every important office in the state—Chief Justice, President of the
Assembly, Lieutenant-Governor. He worked honestly and faithfully
for the Penn family—a cause which grew more and more unpopular
as time went by. His political career was by no means peaceful. He
was often brusque and disdainful in manner and could speak with a
plainness of speech that daunted even his fellow-Quakers. He fought
Lord Baltimore strenuously over the boundaries of Maryland and
Pennsylvania. He opposed Sir William Keith on paper currency. He
shocked the Quakers by favoring a militia for home-defence. At one
time he was even threatened with impeachment but he held calmly
on his way. Somehow he survived all attacks and impressed himself
upon the imagination of his fellow-citizens as a man at once upright,
vigorous, without bitterness and without fear. At length about 1726
he retired from active participation in politics—only now and then
the old lion would reach out a paw and pat the squabbling politicians
—gently but ominously—on the back. He had, in the course of a busy
life spent in other men's service, somehow managed to acquire riches.
He built himself a country-home at Stenton, baking his own bricks
and serving as his own architect, and there he settled down to his
hobbies once more—mathematics, astronomy, botany and gardening.
He corresponded with learned men all over the world and with the
help of his brother in England collected together a library of over
2000 volumes.

Logan was more than a reader of books. He was an author and a
practical scientist, too. Having acquired a working knowledge of the
new Linnæan theory of botany he made experiments in the cultiva-
tion of maize or Indian corn at Stenton. The results he published in a
learned work in Latin, published at Leyden in 1739—*Experimenta et
Meletemata de Plantarum Generatione*. The book was later translated
into English by Dr. John Fothergill and published in London, 1747.
For this and other contributions to their common science Linnæus
greeted Logan as one of the great botanists of the day and named the
shrub *Logania* after him. In 1741 he published another book in Latin
at Leyden—*Demonstrationes de Radiorum Lucis* . . . the fruit of his
astronomical researches. To Sir Hans Sloane and the Royal Society in
London he sent papers on "The Crooked and Angular Appearance of

M. T. CICERO's
CATO MAJOR,
OR HIS
DISCOURSE
OF
OLD-AGE:
With Explanatory NOTES.

PHILADELPHIA:
Printed and Sold by B. FRANKLIN,
MDCCXLIV.

Logan's translation of Cicero's *Dialogue on Old Age*,
pr. by Franklin with a rubricated title-page.

Lightning" and on "The Sun and the Moon, when nearing the Horizon, appearing larger," which were published in the *Philosophical Transactions*. In Philadelphia at Franklin's press he published two books. The first was a translation of Cato's *Moral Distiches* (1735), made for his own sons, the second a translation of Cicero's *Cato Major* (1743) or dialogue on old age, made by Logan, Franklin tells us in the preface, "partly for his own Amusement, being then in his 60th year . . . but principally for the Entertainment of a Neighbor then in his grand Climacteric." These were the first two translations from the Classics to be made and printed in America. The *Cato Major* Franklin printed in a special edition in good clear print on extra fine paper with a rubricated title-page—the finest product of his press. The clear print and the fine paper, he says in the preface, he had used, because those who began to think on the subject of old age too often found their eyesight impaired by its approaches. He afterwards had the book re-printed in London.

Logan was a man of radio-active energy of mind. He could inspire young men with his own intellectual enthusiasms. He it was who made Philadelphia a city of natural philosophers, inventors, botanists and experimental scientists in the eighteenth century—the city, in short, to which young Franklin came when he escaped from the decadent theology of Boston. Franklin and Logan were often divided by differences of political opinion, but each man respected the other and in the interludes of faction they were even friends: Logan quickly recognised Franklin's alert and inventive mind and Franklin owed to Logan his first introduction to experiments in electricity. Thomas Godfrey came to Stenton to glaze windows, but Logan found in him a fellow mathematician, turned him into an inventor and defended his claim with the Royal Society for the invention of the Mariner's Quadrant. Parsons, the cobbler, through his help became a mapmaker and surveyor. And to John Bartram, the farmer of Kingsessing, he lent books upon gardening and agriculture. He introduced him to the work of Linnæus, translated the Latin for him and thus made of him the man whom Linnæus himself was to hail as the greatest practical botanist of the age. The influence of Logan lived long after him. It produced David Rittenhouse, the astronomer, and the honored line of Philadelphia botanists whose fame is forever commemorated in the names of flowers and shrubs, such as *Wistaria*, the wide world over. And it was not by chance random that the Garden Club of America was founded in Logan's city, Philadelphia.

His first library of 800 books Logan had been forced to sell at Dublin on his way out to America. But once more at Stenton he went to work to build up a library. One much prized work that he had been obliged to sacrifice was Ptolemy's *Geography and Almagest* with Theon's commentary in Greek. He hunted for a second copy in vain. Finally he wrote to the learned German scholar, Fabricius, asking him if he knew of any copy. Fabricius took one from his own library that had once belonged to Gronovius, the Dutch botanist, and sent it to Logan, telling him that he was a lucky man—the volume was so scarce that "neither prayers nor price could purchase it." With this as his corner-stone Logan built up a truly remarkable library. A distinguished scholar from Europe was found slapping and pinching himself one day among the mathematical and astronomical books. "Am I dreaming?" he exclaimed; "or awake? Some of these books are unprocurable to-day. I have hunted for them in vain in many libraries in Europe. And here they are altogether in America, and here they have been apparently for over two hundred years. Who was this man Logan and how did he know where to look?"

Without giving a list of names of the books that this distinguished mathematician touched with trembling hands we may note that Logan had procured an almost complete set of all the works of Sir Isaac Newton in every edition, which he then had heavily and sagely annotated. He had the works of other contemporary mathematicians—Flamsteed, Halley, Wallis and Jones. But to leave mathematics for other branches of human wisdom, in botany he had procured the works of Linnæus—in first editions bought as soon as they were published—of Gronovius and Charles Plumier and innumerable herbals and botanical "theatres." All the Greek and Latin classics—including Bentley's editions—were there, and Bede's Anglo-Saxon history in Anglo-Saxon type. There were books of the fine and useful arts—Palladio's architecture, Leonardo da Vinci's painting, ship-building, typography. There were the best historians, ancient and modern, books of travel in every known continent and ocean—Dampier's *Voyages* to New Spain and New Holland, Harris' *Collections*, Purchas' *His Pilgrimes*, Ramusio's *Viaggi*, Capt. Smith's *Virginia*, John Ray's *Curious Travels . . . in the Levant*. There were several contemporary English political tracts, written by Steele, Addison, Swift and others —on the title-page of one of Swift's pamphlets Sir William Temple, his old patron, has written his name. There were books given to Logan by William Penn and his sons—with the Penn book-plate still in

them—a *History of the Turks* and a polyglot Bible printed at Nurem-
burg, 1599. In later years Logan became interested in the Spanish Con-
quistadors and missionaries and added works written in Latin, Spanish
and English about the conquest, settlement and christianising of
Mexico, South America and the West Indies—books by Acosta,
Gomara, Herrera and others. English letters he thought of mainly in
terms of age and poetry—they are faithfully represented in his library
by Rowe's *Shakespeare* and Speght's *Chaucer*. With contemporary literature as such he was not much concerned, but those few books that
he did collect reveal the humor of his mind—a few odd writings of
Defoe, Pope's *Dunciad* and several of Swift's works, including the
Tale of a Tub, but not, alas! *Gulliver's Travels*.

To make the round of Logan's books in his library is like making a
tour through his own robust and energetic mind. His signature—in a
beautiful Greek-formed hand—stands invariably as "*J. Logan*" at the
top right-hand corner of each title-page. Many of the books—particularly the mathematical and astronomical books—are annotated in the
same clear and beautiful hand-writing—sometimes in the margin,
sometimes on sheets of paper bound in—sometimes in Latin, once or
twice in Greek, and when he wished to be sarcastic, in English. Logan's
foible was accuracy and more than once Sir Isaac Newton receives
chastisement on that score. On the title-page of some poor work about
comets he has written "a truly invaluable Work, could but the Reader
be assured it was correct." In other volumes his comments are strictly
personal, about the borrowers of his books, not their authors. More
than once he notes that Thomas Godfrey and sometimes his son (pre-
sumably the poet) have "fouled" the margins. On one occasion his
displeasure was so severe that he had to hide Godfrey's shame from
posterity in Latin. He notes on the fly-leaf of Flamsteed's *Historia
Coelestis Britannica* that he had lent the volume to Thomas Godfrey
"*dummodo hic . . . se bene gesserit*" (provided that he . . . behaved
himself properly). But Godfrey somehow had offended, for under this
sentence comes another—"*31 Jan 173⅘. Non ita se gessit, ideoq.
totum istud refigo et irritum reddo* (he hasn't behaved himself thus, so
I cancel all the above and render it void) *J. Logan*."

Most interesting, however, as giving us a glimpse into Logan's mind
is a volume entitled *Hallei Tabulæ Astronomiæ*. This consists of the
proof-sheets of an unpublished book by Edmund Halley of comet
fame. Halley was too poor to publish the work, but he allowed Logan,
when he was in London in 1723–4 to purchase the sheets from William

Innys, his bookseller and printer. The sheets comprise a series of astronomical tables (incomplete), and two treatises in Latin—one on the motions of the satellites of Saturn, the other on the motions of comets. Logan took these sheets back to Stenton. In manuscript he completed the astronomical tables. To the two treatises he subjoined in Latin a few comments of his own and a tentative study of the motions of the moon. Finally he closed, still in Latin, with an account of an eclipse of the sun that he had witnessed on his visit to England in 1723–4. He had gone down from Marlborough to Windsor with John Penn and Thomas Penn, the sons of William Penn, and there, on May 11th, 1724, had followed the eclipse through a telescope from the Castle Terrace. Later he had attended a meeting at the Royal Society when Halley had lectured on the eclipse and, he regretted to say, Halley had, like too many mathematicians that he knew, been somewhat lax in his calculations. Still, says Logan in closing, he had written down his own observations to honor the memory of that *"celeberrimus auctor, Edmundus Halleius."* His final words are *"Haec tremulâ et languidâ ex paralysi manu scripsi 23° Aprilis die an. 1745—"* (This I have written on the 23rd day of April in the year 1745 with a hand tremulous and languid with paralysis.)

James Logan was never the man to hug all his learning to himself. He loved to impart it to other men—particularly to young men. He was anxious that others beside himself should read his books. He therefore erected a small wooden building at the corner of Walnut and Sixth Streets and housed his library there. With proper introductions any citizen of Philadelphia might consult the books and even, on promise of good behavior, take them home. Thither came Ben Franklin, Tom Godfrey, Jack Bartram and many another young man in quest of modern learning that could be found in such plenty nowhere else in the American Colonies at that time. In 1745 Logan executed a design for a more permanent building and in 1749 he left his library of 2000 volumes to "the public" of Philadelphia "in order to prevail on them (having such assistance) to acquaint themselves with literature." As Bodley's library at Oxford was called the Bodleian Library, so his library was to be called the Loganian Library. The family of Logan was always to be connected with it. His eldest son was to be the first Librarian and after him that son's eldest son, and so on down the family tree, first through the male and then through the female line. Every one of these hereditary Librarians must be a classical scholar, capable of understanding the Greek Testament

name ofte Andʐ by cause þrof þhan he
was dedeʐ they that þrdʐ thyse wordes
openedʐ hys body & drewe out his þr
te & cut it openʐ Andʐ they fonde wryth
in the name of Iʒhu wreton wyth
fayr lettres of goldʐ /   For whyche
myracle many retruedʐ þe fayth of
Iʒhu cryst /   Of thys saynt sayth
saynt bernardʐ vpon the psalme /
Qui þabitat / Saynt Ignace martir
of godʐ glorpous is of grete merpte /
whyche was mynyster to the dyscyple
that Iʒhus so moche louydʐ / Andʐ in
hys eppstles / the whyche he sente to
the glorpous vyrgyne marpe / he sale &
wedʐ þer as moder that hadʐ born Iʒhu

cryst / Andʐ þr rsaluedʐ hym agayn
in fygne that he was a persone of grete
honour / of grete dygnyte / andʐ of
of grete Auctorpte /The body of whom
was honourably burpedʐ of crysten mē
to the worshyppe of Iʒhu cryst / whiche
is blessydʐ in secula seculorum Amen /

Here endeth the lyf of saynt Ignacien

And here foloweth the purpfica­cion of our lady

POstquam impleti
sunt dies purgacionis
marie secundum legem
mopsi tulerunt Iʒhsum in
Iʒherusalem /luce secundo
capitulo / Thauncyent
lawe had his cource vntil the tyme that
god hath suffredʐ deth for vs / Andʐ
whan he deyde on the crosse / þe saydʐ
Iohannis nono capto / Consummatum
est / That is to saye / alle thyngʐ is fp
npsshed and ended that hath be wreten
of me whyche lawe he kepte durynge
hys lpf / as it is wreten / I am not

comen for to breke the lawe / In whych
he gaf vs example of humplyte / and
of obedience /lpke as saynt þoul saith
In lpke wyse our lady for toþepe to
the lawe / bare þer swete sone Iʒhsu
Cryst vnto the temple of Iʒherusalem af­
ter the xl dayes of hys byrthe / for to
offre hym to godʐ / andʐ for to gyue
offrynge for hym suche as in the lawe
was ordeynedʐ / that is to wete a
payr turtellis / or two dowues was
thoffrynge of poure folke / lpke as
it is wreten /   Our lordʐ
whyche in alle was cam to maþe our

r iij

and the poems of Hesiod and Homer in the original tongue. If, however, no Logan could be found with the necessary qualifications, then the trustees were "without hesitation to appoint such a proficient in literature, if he be at the same time of a sober life and conversation."

There was some delay in putting Logan's wishes into effect after his death in 1751 and for many years the building on Walnut Street was closed. But Dr. William Logan, the son of James, had inherited his father's love of books and continued to add to the library—such works as the Baskerville *Bible* and finely printed editions of Greek and Latin comedies. In 1760 a catalogue of the books was printed. In that year, too, Dr. Logan drew up a Deed of Trust with the Library Company, making it a trustee of his father's library. But again there was unaccountable delay. The Revolutionary War broke out and Dr. Logan died and still the Loganian Library was not open to the public. It was not until 1792 that the Library Company finally took over the trust. In the Deed it was ordained that there should be three Loganian Trustees to serve as co-trustees with the Directors of the Library Company. One of these trustees was to be the eldest male descendant in the male line from James Logan living within a seven mile radius of the City of Philadelphia. That trustee is to-day Mr. Robert Logan.

The Loganian Library was housed in the outer room of the Library Building on Fifth Street. Moreau de St. Mèry visited it there in 1794 and says that it then had 5000 volumes. In 1795 Zachariah Poulson published a second catalogue. When the Library Company vacated the Fifth Street building in 1880 the Loganian Library was moved to the upper gallery of the Ridgway Branch.

During the first ten years of its life with the Library Company the Loganian Library had a generous friend in William Mackenzie. Very little is known of this benefactor. He was "a gentleman," say the *Directories*, and lived on High Street. He seems to have been wealthy and was a friend of Washington in his Presidential days. His portrait —by John Neagle—reveals to us a very charming personage—a handsome, youthful-looking man, very much "the gentleman," with a powdered wig and an alert and humorous face. He is seated in a red velvet arm-chair, with a large folio volume propped upon his knee to show which way his humor ran. He loved books for books' sake—for their paper, their type, their bindings, their age and only incidentally for their authors and subject matter. Among his gifts to the Loganian Library were a Book of Hours, printed on vellum by *Vèrard* (*Paris, 1508*), lavishly illustrated in color, Dante's *Divina Comedia*, printed at

Venice by Benali and Mattheo di Parma, 1491, illustrated with wood-cuts, and "the glory of the Jensen press," Pliny's *Historia Naturalis* printed at Venice, 1472, on vellum with illuminated borders and initial letters and presented to Don Lodovico of Aragon, grandson of Ferdi-nand, King of Naples. And last but not least we must mention Voragine's *Golden Legend* (Lon. 1483)—the first Caxton to come to American shores. Though he loved old books Mackenzie was not blind to the charms of contemporary literature or of rare *Americana*. When he died he left several books to the Library Company. Among them was a first edition of Byron's *Childe Harold*, *Canto IV*, still in the original boards, and Francis Rawle's *Ways and Means for the Inhabitants of Delaware to become Rich* (Phila. 1725)— the first treatise on political economy ever written in America and the first book that Franklin himself set up in type.

To-day the Loganian Library numbers about 15,000 volumes. It boasts a remarkable collection of books on gardening, costume, art, silverware, pewter, architecture and furniture collected together by a former assistant Librarian, Miss Elisabeth McClellan.